ALSO BY SARAH, THE DUCHESS OF YORK

The Palace of Westminster

Victoria and Albert:
Life at Osborne House

Travels with Queen Victoria

My Story

ALSO BY WEIGHT WATCHERS

Coach Approach:
How to Motivate the "Thin" You

Simply the Best:
250 Prizewinning Family Recipes

Versatile Vegetarian:
150 Easy Recipes for Every Day

. . . and many more

Dining with The Duchess

MAKING EVERYDAY MEALS
A SPECIAL OCCASION

◆

Sarah, The Duchess of York
and
Weight Watchers

Simon & Schuster

SIMON & SCHUSTER
Rockefeller Center
1230 Avenue of the Americas
New York, NY 10020

DESIGNED BY DEBORAH KERNER
Manufactured in the United States of America
3   5   7   9   10   8   6   4

Library of Congress Cataloging-in-Publication Data is available.

ISBN 0-684-84915-1

A WORD ABOUT WEIGHT WATCHERS

Since 1963, Weight Watchers has grown from a handful of people to millions of enrollments annually. Today, Weight Watchers is recognized as the leading name in safe and sensible weight control. Weight Watchers members form diverse groups, from youths to senior citizens, attending meetings virtually around the globe. Weight-loss and weight-management results vary by individual, but we recommend that you attend Weight Watchers meetings, follow the Weight Watchers food plan and participate in regular physical activity. For the Weight Watchers meeting nearest you, call 1-800-651-6000.

WEIGHT WATCHERS PUBLISHING GROUP
EDITORIAL DIRECTOR: NANCY GAGLIARDI
SENIOR EDITOR: MARTHA SCHUENEMAN
ASSOCIATE EDITOR: CHRISTINE SENFT, M.S.
RECIPE DEVELOPERS: REGINA RAGONE, M.S., R.D., MAUREEN LUCHEJKO,
BARRY BLUESTEIN, AND KEVIN MORRISSEY
NUTRITION CONSULTANT: MINDY HERMANN, M.B.A., R.D.
PHOTOGRAPHER: RITA MAAS
FOOD STYLIST: MARIANN SAUVION
PROP STYLIST: VALORIE FISHER

Contents

Contents

6

Contents

7

Recipes not included.

Introduction

By now, the world over has heard my story: When it was first announced that I would be marrying Prince Andrew, the British press greeted me with open arms, calling me "Great Fun Fergie, a breath of fresh air." Yet the moment I began gaining weight, that very same press turned on me, calling me "Fat Fergie" which gave way to "Fat and Appalling Fergie" and ultimately, "The Duchess of Pork."

While I can laugh at those names today, it is no surprise that at the time I felt humiliated, alone, defeated. When my life was out of control, so was my weight. At times, I felt as if I was on a downward spiral, spinning faster and faster.

I have since learned that those dismal feelings I had were not unlike the emotions experienced by almost everyone who has done battle with his or her weight. Losing weight and trying to maintain a fit body and healthy lifestyle truly is one of life's great challenges. Yet I have also learned that rock bottom can be a powerful place from where to restart one's life. There's no place to go but up.

In the past year, I have learned a tremendous amount about eating the right foods, exercising and banishing bad habits. I have learned these lessons from women who have refused to become victims: my old friends, my new friends at Weight Watchers, and health and fitness experts I have met in my travels. Happily, I can call on these people when I need them most. They are my support network.

At the first thought of doing a cookbook, I was skeptical, to say the least. First of all, I very rarely cook, given my hectic schedule. When I was a single working girl living in London, I tended to live on student staples like baked beans on toast or whatever I could find in the fridge. Once I was married, I was unable to cook for myself and my husband because our apartment at Buckingham Palace did not have a kitchen.

Today, I am lucky enough to employ a cook who knows my likes and dislikes. Yet, in the past year, I have given her a whole new list of favorite foods because my tastes and habits have changed.

Now, instead of simply giving in to my penchant for sausage rolls and mayonnaise, I seek out food that is good for my body. My cook and I discuss menus together, and then she creates in the kitchen. Given my mad travel schedule, I need to know that there is somewhere, a home base, where I can go and refuel my body as well as my soul.

This collection of delicious and healthy recipes masterfully blends the tastes of the old Sarah with the knowledge of the new Sarah. I have based the menus on favorite dishes from my childhood, my travels and some memorable meals I have shared with my family and friends.

Nowadays, food is not the enemy. I am not fearful of every forkful. Rather, I now use food as a way to control my life. I recognize that fresh, wholesome foods will keep me steady and energized. I still enjoy my ham sandwiches, but now I know I can have a little and still maintain control.

I know now that if I can control my weight and food intake, it changes my mood for the day.

It is comforting to know that you can rearrange your thinking and readjust your habits, that you can change. I am happy to say that I have changed. Rock bottom seems like a long time ago. Nowadays, I rather like the view from up here.

SARAH, THE DUCHESS OF YORK

Dining with The Duchess

◆

A Weekend Lunch with Friends

Perhaps one of the greatest challenges I have encountered while trying to lose weight and start a healthier lifestyle is to change my old habits. In the past, when things were going badly or I hit a rough patch, my natural inclination was to eat. My weaknesses are French breads with butter, croissants, sausage rolls (sausages wrapped in buttery puff pastry) and egg and mayonnaise sandwiches, which I think are just delicious. These foods are still my triggers, but I have worked hard at trying to keep my food goblins at bay. I've also worked hard at changing the habits I've developed over a lifetime, and I know how truly difficult that can be. But the results are well worth the sacrifice. Now I am learning that I can be around food and not feel literally consumed by it.

Serves 4

Classic Bloody Marys

Genoa Canapés

Classic Vegetable Frittata

Baked Chicken with Wine

Light Cheese Popovers

Ginger Pears

Mulled Peaches

Classic Bloody Marys

Makes 4 servings

One 32-ounce bottle (4 cups) tomato juice
1 cup vodka
¼ cup fresh lemon juice
2 teaspoons Worcestershire sauce
2 teaspoons prepared horseradish
½ teaspoon celery salt
½ teaspoon hot red pepper sauce
Freshly ground pepper, to taste
4 celery stalks, with leaves

In a large pitcher, mix the tomato juice, vodka, lemon juice, Worcestershire sauce, horseradish, celery salt, pepper sauce and ground pepper. Pour into tall glasses over ice; garnish with the celery stalks.

Per serving: 186 Calories, 1 g Total Fat, 0 g Saturated Fat, 1 mg Cholesterol, 1,188 mg Sodium, 13 g Total Carbohydrate, 2 g Dietary Fiber, 2 g Protein, 42 mg Calcium.

POINTS PER SERVING: 3

Tip

To make a Classic Virgin Mary, omit the vodka; you'll save almost 130 calories and 2 **POINTS**. If you're concerned about your salt intake, use low-sodium tomato juice.

Genoa Canapés

Makes 4 servings

12 slices light rye cocktail bread (3″ squares), halved diagonally
1 tablespoon Dijon mustard
6 paper-thin slices Genoa salami, cut in half

Spread the bread with the mustard. Fold a piece of salami over the bread.

Per serving: 112 CALORIES, 6 G TOTAL FAT, 2 G SATURATED FAT, 13 MG CHOLESTEROL, 381 MG SODIUM, 12 G TOTAL CARBOHYDRATE, 0 G DIETARY FIBER, 5 G PROTEIN, 27 MG CALCIUM.

POINTS PER SERVING: 3

Tip

For a change of pace, try smoked trout or salmon instead of the salami; use prepared horseradish or dill butter in place of the mustard.

Classic Vegetable Frittata

Makes 4 servings

4 eggs

1 cup fat-free egg substitute

½ teaspoon salt

¼ teaspoon freshly ground pepper

¼ teaspoon dried oregano, crumbled

1 teaspoon olive oil

2 onions, chopped

1 red bell pepper, seeded and chopped

1 cup sliced mushrooms

Half 10-ounce bag triple-washed spinach,
rinsed (do not dry) and chopped

1. In a medium bowl, lightly beat the eggs; whisk in the egg substitute, salt, pepper and oregano.
2. In a medium nonstick skillet, heat the oil. Sauté the onions, bell pepper and mushrooms until the onions are golden brown, about 8 minutes. Reduce the heat to low; add the spinach and cook, stirring frequently, until it wilts, about 4 minutes. Stir in the egg mixture; cook, covered, until the eggs are set, 10–13 minutes. Invert the frittata onto a plate and cut into quarters. Serve hot or at room temperature.

Per serving: 164 CALORIES, 7 G TOTAL FAT, 2 G SATURATED FAT, 212 MG CHOLESTEROL, 462 MG SODIUM, 12 G TOTAL CARBOHYDRATE, 3 G DIETARY FIBER, 15 G PROTEIN, 102 MG CALCIUM.

POINTS PER SERVING: 3

Tip

To get that wonderful brown top, preheat the broiler when you add the eggs to the vegetables; cook the frittata on the stove 9–10 minutes, then uncover the skillet and run under the broiler for a minute or so. If your skillet doesn't have an ovenproof handle, wrap the handle in a few layers of foil.

Baked Chicken with Wine

Makes 4 servings

2 tablespoons fresh lemon juice
1 teaspoon minced thyme
½ teaspoon minced rosemary
½ teaspoon salt
½ teaspoon coarsely ground pepper
Four 4-ounce skinless boneless chicken breasts
½ cup dry white wine

1. Preheat the oven to 425° F; spray a 7 x 11″ baking dish with nonstick cooking spray. In a small bowl, mix the lemon juice, thyme, rosemary, salt and pepper.
2. Rub the lemon mixture onto each breast. Place the chicken in the baking dish; pour in the wine. Bake, basting occasionally with the pan juices, until browned and cooked through, about 20 minutes. Serve, drizzled with any pan juices.

Per serving: 147 Calories, 3 g Total Fat, 1 g Saturated Fat, 72 mg Cholesterol, 313 mg Sodium, 2 g Total Carbohydrate, 0 g Dietary Fiber, 26 g Protein, 20 mg Calcium.

POINTS PER SERVING: 3

Tip

Speedy and simple, this family favorite is delicious teamed with Parsley Rice (page 49). Serve with a light Chardonnay or Sauvignon Blanc.

Light Cheese Popovers

Makes 4 servings

⅔ cup skim milk
½ cup + 2 tablespoons all-purpose flour
2 teaspoons olive oil
¼ teaspoon salt
¼ teaspoon freshly ground pepper
Pinch cayenne pepper
2 eggs, beaten
⅓ cup shredded extra-sharp cheddar cheese
2 tablespoons grated Parmesan cheese

1. Preheat the oven to 450° F; spray a shiny aluminum 12-cup muffin tin with nonstick cooking spray.
2. In a medium bowl, whisk the milk, flour, oil, salt, pepper and cayenne; whisk in the eggs.
3. Spoon about 1 tablespoon of batter into each muffin cup; sprinkle with the cheddar and Parmesan, then top with the remaining batter. Bake 15 minutes; reduce the oven temperature to 350° F and bake until the tops of the popovers are golden brown, about 15 minutes longer. Serve warm.

Per serving: 203 CALORIES, 10 G TOTAL FAT, 4 G SATURATED FAT, 120 MG CHOLESTEROL, 301 MG SODIUM, 18 G TOTAL CARBOHYDRATE, 1 G DIETARY FIBER, 10 G PROTEIN, 179 MG CALCIUM.

POINTS PER SERVING: 5

Tip

Be sure to use a shiny muffin tin, since a dark tin may cause the popovers to burn. Be liberal with the cayenne if you prefer spicy foods.

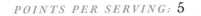

Ginger Pears

Makes 4 servings

4 pears, cored and halved
1 tablespoon minced crystallized ginger
1 tablespoon ginger marmalade

Cut a thin slice from the skin side of the pears so they lie flat; place in a shallow 1-quart microwavable dish. Fill the cavities of the pears with the ginger and marmalade; sprinkle with 2 tablespoons water. Cover the dish with wax paper and microwave on High 3 minutes, then baste the pears with the pan juices; microwave on High until tender, 1 minute longer. Serve, drizzled with the pan juices.

Per serving: 118 Calories, 1 g Total Fat, 0 g Saturated Fat, 0 mg Cholesterol, 5 mg Sodium, 30 g Total Carbohydrate, 4 g Dietary Fiber, 1 g Protein, 28 mg Calcium.

POINTS PER SERVING: 2

Tip

Ginger marmalade imparts a tangy, sophisticated flavor. It is available in most specialty shops and better supermarkets.

Mulled Peaches

Makes 4 servings

2 cups fruity red wine
¼ cup sugar
1 cinnamon stick, cracked
1 teaspoon allspice berries
3–4 whole cloves
4 peaches, halved and pitted
1 orange, sliced

1. In a medium saucepan, combine the wine, sugar, cinnamon, allspice and cloves, stirring until the sugar dissolves; bring to a boil. Reduce the heat and add the peaches and orange; simmer, spooning the cooking liquid over the fruit, until tender, 15–20 minutes.
2. Transfer the fruit to dessert bowls; discard the spices. Pour the mulled wine over the fruit.

Per serving: 186 CALORIES, 0 G TOTAL FAT, 0 G SATURATED FAT, 0 MG CHOLESTEROL, 6 MG SODIUM, 28 G TOTAL CARBOHYDRATE, 3 G DIETARY FIBER, 1 G PROTEIN, 27 MG CALCIUM.

POINTS PER SERVING: 3

Tip

Merlot, Gamay Beaujolais or Sauternes (if you prefer white wine) would be a good choice in wine. Nectarines or fresh plums can be used in place of the peaches. If you like, spoon on a dollop of nonfat whipped dairy topping.

Writer's Respite

From an early age, I have always enjoyed reading—poetry and prose—and writing. The latter is one medium where I can channel my thoughts and imagination. I love creating with words on a page; then, of course, I have a sense of achievement when a book has come off press.

When I was single, I worked in publishing. Once I was married, it seemed only natural that I gravitate back to writing: The first work I assembled was *The Palace of Westminster*, a coffee-table book on the history of this great palace, with lots of up-to-date photographs. Then I cowrote *Victoria and Albert: Life at Osborne House*, a book filled with wonderful photographs that showcased the royal couple's life. The following book, *Travels with Queen Victoria*, was a high point in my publishing career; it truly was a labor of love as I retraced the Queen's travels at the end of the nineteenth century. I tried to recapture the sights and sounds she experienced so the reader could as well.

Today, writing is something I love. It's hard work and hardly for the meek. But I always discover something new about myself when I'm working on a new project.

Serves 4

Ginger-Carrot Soup

Spinach Salad with Tangy Orange Dressing

Crusty Bread*

Vanilla-Poached Fruit

Pot of Tea*

Ginger-Carrot Soup

Makes 4 servings

3 carrots, scrubbed and thinly sliced
2 cups chicken broth
2 teaspoons minced peeled gingerroot
2 garlic cloves, minced
¼ teaspoon freshly ground pepper
¼ teaspoon ground allspice
1 cup low-fat (1%) milk

In a large saucepan or Dutch oven, combine the carrots, broth, gingerroot, garlic, pepper and allspice; bring to a boil. Reduce the heat and simmer until the carrots are tender, about 10 minutes. Transfer to a blender; add the milk and puree. Return to the saucepan and cook, stirring, until heated through, 2–3 minutes; do not let the soup boil.

Per serving: 69 CALORIES, 2 G TOTAL FAT, 1 G SATURATED FAT, 12 MG CHOLESTEROL, 545 MG SODIUM, 10 G TOTAL CARBOHYDRATE, 2 G DIETARY FIBER, 4 G PROTEIN, 94 MG CALCIUM.

POINTS PER SERVING: 1

Tip

Be careful peeling gingerroot—its knobs are prime slipping areas for knives and vegetable peelers.

Spinach Salad
with Tangy Orange Dressing

Makes 4 servings

2 tablespoons orange juice

4 teaspoons balsamic vinegar

1 tablespoon sugar

1 tablespoon olive oil

¼ teaspoon salt

¼ teaspoon freshly ground pepper

One 10-ounce bag triple-washed spinach, rinsed and
torn into bite-size pieces

2 cups sliced mushrooms

3 slices bacon, crisp-cooked and crumbled

1 red onion, thinly sliced

1. In a small bowl, whisk the orange juice, vinegar, sugar, oil, salt and pepper.
2. In a large salad bowl, mix the spinach, mushrooms, bacon and onion. Drizzle
    with the dressing; toss to coat.

Per serving: 114 Calories, 6 g Total Fat, 1 g Saturated Fat, 4 mg Cholesterol,
269 mg Sodium, 12 g Total Carbohydrate, 3 g Dietary Fiber, 5 g Protein,
82 mg Calcium.

POINTS PER SERVING: 2

Tip

For tangy lemon or lime dressing, substitute lemon or lime juice for the o.j.
and cut the vinegar to 2 teaspoons; add more vinegar to taste.

Vanilla-Poached Fruit

Makes 4 servings

1 lemon
¼ cup sugar
One 2″ length vanilla bean, split
2 pears, peeled, cored and cut into wedges
2 Granny Smith apples, peeled, cored and cut into wedges
¼ cup dried cranberries or raisins

1. With a zester or vegetable peeler, remove the zest from the lemon in long strips; place in a medium saucepan. Squeeze the lemon juice into the saucepan. Add the sugar, vanilla bean and 1 cup water, stirring until the sugar dissolves; bring to a boil. Reduce the heat and simmer 5 minutes.
2. Add the pears, apples and cranberries to the poaching liquid; simmer, spooning the poaching liquid over the fruit, until tender, about 10 minutes longer.
3. With a slotted spoon, transfer the fruit to a medium bowl; discard the vanilla bean. Simmer the liquid, stirring occasionally, until thick and syrupy, about 5 minutes; pour over the fruit.

Per serving: 140 CALORIES, 0 G TOTAL FAT, 0 G SATURATED FAT, 0 MG CHOLESTEROL, 3 MG SODIUM, 37 G TOTAL CARBOHYDRATE, 3 G DIETARY FIBER, 1 G PROTEIN, 12 MG CALCIUM.

POINTS PER SERVING: 2

Tip

This is every bit as delicious cold. Refrigerate any leftovers to enjoy for breakfast with vanilla nonfat yogurt.

A Highlands Picnic

When things get particularly trying or my schedule is hectic (which is always!), I would eat to soothe my frazzled soul but seldom to satisfy my hunger. To offset this, I have found what I call my "tonics." My children, obviously, are my number one tonic. Spending time with them always helps me put things in perspective. Skiing and riding are tonics for my body; painting and writing, tonics for my soul.

Nature also is a tonic, particularly the mountains. Balmoral, the castle in the Scottish Highlands which is the Royal Family's summer home, was the perfect retreat. I will always treasure the time I spent there, walking in the rolling hills or sitting on the banks of the River Dee. The Highlands are an idyllic sanctuary. I love immersing myself in the total sense of isolation. Moving the body and the mind, I have found, are critical for happiness, as well as good health. My trainer and friend Josh Saltzman has been a great encouragement and has reiterated my theory, "Free your mind, and the weight will follow."

Serves 4

Easy Cream of Tomato Soup

Mediterranean Tuna Salad

Mesquite Chicken Salad

Honey-Orange Biscotti

Fuji and Granny Smith Apples*

Easy Cream of Tomato Soup

Makes 4 servings

2 cups skim milk

1 tablespoon all-purpose flour

¾ teaspoon salt

4 tomatoes, coarsely chopped

¼ onion, coarsely chopped

1 tablespoon coarsely chopped parsley

1 teaspoon sugar

¼ teaspoon freshly ground pepper

2 teaspoons Worcestershire sauce (optional)

1. In a medium saucepan over low heat, combine the milk, flour and ½ teaspoon of the salt; cook, stirring almost constantly, until thickened, about 5 minutes.
2. Meanwhile, in a blender or food processor, combine the tomatoes, onion, parsley, sugar, pepper, Worcestershire sauce (if using) and the remaining ¼ teaspoon of salt; puree. Place a large sieve over the saucepan; slowly pour the pureed tomatoes into the milk mixture, pressing with a wooden spoon. Cook, stirring constantly, until heated through, 2–3 minutes; do not let the soup boil.

Per serving: 83 CALORIES, 1 G TOTAL FAT, 0 G SATURATED FAT, 2 MG CHOLESTEROL, 475 MG SODIUM, 15 G TOTAL CARBOHYDRATE, 2 G DIETARY FIBER, 6 G PROTEIN, 164 MG CALCIUM.

POINTS PER SERVING: 1

Tip

For a main-dish soup, toss in some diced ham; serve with Spicy Polenta (page 56) or Herbed Parmesan Biscuits (page 181) on the side. Pressing the tomatoes through a sieve strains the peels and seeds, yielding a smooth, creamy texture.

Mediterranean Tuna Salad

Makes 4 servings

1 cup orzo

Two 6-ounce cans solid white water-packed tuna,
drained and flaked

1 celery stalk, minced

¼ cup minced flat-leaf parsley

3 scallions, sliced

2 tablespoons fresh lemon juice

¼ teaspoon salt

¼ teaspoon coarsely ground pepper

8 green-leaf lettuce leaves

1. Cook the orzo according to package directions; drain and place in a serving
   bowl. Stir in the tuna, celery, parsley, scallions, lemon juice, salt and pepper.
   Refrigerate, covered, until the flavors are blended, at least 2 hours.
2. Divide the lettuce among 4 salad plates; top with the salad.

Per serving: 316 CALORIES, 2 G TOTAL FAT, 0 G SATURATED FAT, 26 MG CHOLESTEROL,
436 MG SODIUM, 44 G TOTAL CARBOHYDRATE, 2 G DIETARY FIBER, 29 G PROTEIN,
34 MG CALCIUM.

POINTS PER SERVING: 6

Tip

If you like, serve this classic summertime salad in the classic warm-weather
way: stuffed into scooped-out tomatoes.

Mesquite Chicken Salad

Makes 4 servings

2 tablespoons fresh lemon juice

1 tablespoon olive oil

¼ teaspoon freshly ground pepper

¼ teaspoon mustard powder

Pinch salt

One 8-ounce package skinless mesquite-flavored cooked
chicken breasts, diced

12 cherry tomatoes, halved

1 yellow bell pepper, seeded and diced

1 red onion, diced

8 radicchio leaves

1. In a small bowl, whisk the lemon juice, oil, pepper, mustard powder and salt.
2. In a large bowl, mix the chicken, tomatoes, bell pepper and onion. Drizzle with the dressing; toss to coat. Refrigerate, covered, until the flavors are blended, at least 2 hours.
3. Divide the radicchio among 4 salad plates; top with the salad.

Per serving: 129 CALORIES, 4 G TOTAL FAT, 1 G SATURATED FAT, 25 MG CHOLESTEROL, 241 MG SODIUM, 12 G TOTAL CARBOHYDRATE, 2 G DIETARY FIBER, 13 G PROTEIN, 23 MG CALCIUM.

POINTS PER SERVING: 3

Tip

If your supermarket's refrigerator poultry case doesn't have mesquite-flavor chicken breasts, check the deli counter for mesquite-smoked turkey breast. If you run out of luck in both places, stir in ½–1 teaspoon mesquite-flavored liquid smoke with the other dressing ingredients.

Honey-Orange Biscotti

Makes 42 servings

3 cups all-purpose flour

1 tablespoon cinnamon

1 teaspoon baking soda

¾ teaspoon baking powder

½ teaspoon ground allspice

¼ teaspoon salt

½ cup golden raisins

½ cup finely chopped dried apricots

2 teaspoons grated orange zest

½ cup sugar

½ cup honey

2 egg whites

1 egg

1. Adjust the racks to divide the oven into thirds. Preheat the oven to 325° F; spray 2 large nonstick baking sheets with nonstick cooking spray.
2. In a large bowl, combine the flour, cinnamon, baking soda, baking powder, allspice and salt; stir in the raisins, apricots and orange zest. In a medium bowl, whisk the sugar, honey, egg whites, egg and 2 tablespoons water. Add to the dry ingredients, stirring until combined.
3. On a lightly floured surface, divide the dough into fourths and form each into a 15″ log. Place 2 logs on each baking sheet, with space in between. Bake, reversing the baking sheets once, until golden brown and firm to the touch, about 25 minutes. Reduce the oven temperature to 250° F.
4. While the logs are hot, transfer to a cutting board. With a serrated knife, cut on the diagonal into ⅜″ slices, making 84 biscotti. Place the slices upright on the baking sheets, 1″ apart. Bake the biscotti until the cut sides feel just dry to

the touch, 15–20 minutes (the biscotti will crisp and dry completely upon cooling). Cool completely on wire racks. Store in an airtight container.

Per serving: 70 Calories, 0 g Total Fat, 0 g Saturated Fat, 5 mg Cholesterol, 57 mg Sodium, 16 g Total Carbohydrate , 1 g Dietary Fiber, 1 g Protein, 15 mg Calcium.

POINTS PER SERVING: 1

_____ *Tip* _____

Most ovens have "hot spots," so it's important to reverse the baking sheets so that the biscotti cook evenly. Give each sheet a half-turn, and switch them top-to-bottom as well.

After-Workout Reviver

I won't lie and tell you I am mad about exercise. While I do enjoy activities like riding and skiing, working out at the local gym can be, at times, impossible. But over the years, I have learned that my body needs to move about. Fit body, fit mind is how I see it.

I now know what works for me. For instance, I know that exercising first thing in the morning invigorates me and sets me straight for the day ahead.

When I am home, I work out at least three times a week with my personal trainer, Josh, at a health club. If I am going out to dinner in the evening or want to allow myself a pudding or treat, I often spend an extra 30 minutes on the exercise bike. When I am away on business trips, I rarely have a moment to exercise—a fact I am fully aware of. When I can, I do climb the steps (it drives my security men mad!) or step up on a piece of furniture (a footstool does the trick) in my hotel room so I can keep on working.

Serves 4

Red Snapper Primavera

Lemon Capellini

Fresh Mesclun* with Basic Vinaigrette

Red Snapper Primavera

Makes 4 servings

Four 6-ounce red snapper fillets
½ teaspoon salt
¼ teaspoon freshly ground pepper
1 red bell pepper, seeded and thinly sliced
1 medium yellow squash, julienned
½ small leek, cleaned and julienned
1 carrot, julienned
¼ cup dry white wine
4 teaspoons fresh lemon juice

1. Preheat the oven to 425° F; lightly spray four 12 x 18″ sheets of foil with non-stick cooking spray. Place a fillet in the center of each sheet; season with the salt and pepper. Top with the vegetables; sprinkle with the wine and lemon juice. Make packets by bringing the sides of the foil up to meet in the center and folding over the edges, then folding the edges of the ends together. Allowing room for the packets to expand, crimp the edges together.

2. Bake the packets until the fish is opaque, about 10 minutes; open the packets carefully when testing for doneness, as steam will escape. Serve, drizzled with any juices that collect in the packets.

Per serving: 189 Calories, 3 g Total Fat, 0 g Saturated Fat, 52 mg Cholesterol, 378 mg Sodium, 7 g Total Carbohydrate, 2 g Dietary Fiber, 30 g Protein, 76 mg Calcium.

POINTS PER SERVING: 4

Tip

Use this technique, known as *en papillote*, with different ingredients—try salmon instead of the snapper, or snow peas instead of the peppers.

Lemon Capellini

Makes 4 servings

6 ounces capellini
2 teaspoons olive oil
1–2 garlic cloves, minced
¼ cup minced parsley
2 tablespoons fresh lemon juice
¼ teaspoon salt
Freshly ground pepper, to taste

1. Cook the capellini according to package directions; drain.
2. Meanwhile, in a large nonstick skillet over medium-low heat, heat the oil. Sauté the garlic until it turns a rich, nutty brown, 2–3 minutes (take care to keep the heat fairly low so the garlic doesn't scorch). Add the capellini, parsley, lemon juice and salt; toss to coat. Serve, sprinkled with the pepper.

Per serving: 183 CALORIES, 3 G TOTAL FAT, 0 G SATURATED FAT, 0 MG CHOLESTEROL, 140 MG SODIUM, 33 G TOTAL CARBOHYDRATE, 1 G DIETARY FIBER, 6 G PROTEIN, 16 MG CALCIUM.

POINTS PER SERVING: 4

Tip

Fine angel-hair pasta complements the delicate lemon flavor of this dish. If you're looking for an extra kick, sprinkle on a few chopped anchovies (a little-known source of heart-healthy Omega-3 fatty acids) before serving.

Basic Vinaigrette

Makes 6 servings

2 tablespoons extra virgin olive oil
2 tablespoons red-wine vinegar
2 teaspoons balsamic vinegar
½ teaspoon Dijon mustard
Pinch salt

In a small bowl, whisk all the ingredients with 1 tablespoon water.

Per serving: 42 CALORIES, 5 G TOTAL FAT, 1 G SATURATED FAT, 0 MG CHOLESTEROL,
24 MG SODIUM, 1 G TOTAL CARBOHYDRATE, 0 G DIETARY FIBER, 0 G PROTEIN,
1 MG CALCIUM.

POINTS PER SERVING: 1

Tip

This dressing keeps in the refrigerator for about a week. If you'll be serving it right away, mix it in the salad bowl and add the greens to it; if you'll be keeping it awhile, shake it in a small jar.

Quick and Easy Family Dinner

I write a syndicated column that appears in newspapers across the country. Each week, I write about the subjects that are closest to my heart: children and helping the less fortunate children round the world, my travels and the challenges I face living the life of a working mother while trying to stay healthy.

Even though things often feel quite hectic, now that I am at a healthy weight, I've found that I am becoming more confident. The more I can control my weight, the more I can control my life and the more I can get out there with confidence and do what needs to be done.

Serves 4

Steak Frites

Corn Salsa

Cucumber Relish

Minted Zucchini

Frozen Yogurt Sundaes

Steak Frites

Makes 4 servings

2 large baking potatoes, scrubbed and cut into ¼″ sticks

2 egg whites

½ teaspoon salt

½ teaspoon freshly ground pepper

3 shallots, minced

4 garlic cloves, minced

One 1-pound lean boneless sirloin steak (1″ thick)

¼ cup steak sauce

1. Preheat the oven to 425° F; spray a nonstick baking sheet with nonstick cooking spray. In a large bowl, combine the potatoes, egg whites, salt and ¼ teaspoon of the pepper; toss to coat. Transfer to the baking sheet. Bake until the potatoes are barely tender, about 15 minutes. Remove the potatoes from the oven and increase the oven temperature to broil.

2. Spray the broiler rack with nonstick cooking spray. In a small bowl, mix the shallots, garlic and the remaining ¼ teaspoon of pepper. Place the steak on the rack; brush on one side with half the steak sauce. Broil 4″ from heat 4 minutes; turn over and brush with the remaining steak sauce. With a fork, press the shallot mixture into the steak; broil until cooked through, about 3 minutes longer. Let the steak stand 10 minutes before slicing.

3. While the steak stands, return the potatoes to the broiler; broil until crispy, about 10 minutes.

Per serving: 374 CALORIES, 8 G TOTAL FAT, 3 G SATURATED FAT, 57 MG CHOLESTEROL, 578 MG SODIUM, 44 G TOTAL CARBOHYDRATE, 4 G DIETARY FIBER, 32 G PROTEIN, 29 MG CALCIUM.

POINTS PER SERVING: 7

Continued on next page.

This is classic French bistro fare. If you can't find shallots, substitute a small onion. If you prefer to grill the steak, don't let the fries sit between baking and broiling—just increase the oven temperature.

Corn Salsa

Makes 4 servings

1½ cups fresh or thawed frozen corn kernels
1 tomato, chopped
1 onion, chopped
1 tablespoon chopped cilantro
1 tablespoon fresh lime juice
½ teaspoon salt

In a medium bowl, combine all the ingredients. Refrigerate, covered, until the flavors are blended, at least 1 hour.

Per serving: 70 CALORIES, 0 G TOTAL FAT, 0 G SATURATED FAT, 0 MG CHOLESTEROL, 274 MG SODIUM, 17 G TOTAL CARBOHYDRATE, 2 G DIETARY FIBER, 2 G PROTEIN, 13 MG CALCIUM.

POINTS PER SERVING: 1

Tip

This colorful salsa is a tasty accompaniment for most simple main dishes; try it with grilled burgers, poultry, pork or fish. Turn it into a hearty salad by stirring in some black beans.

Cucumber Relish

Makes 4 servings

2 cucumbers, peeled, seeded and diced
2 tomatoes, seeded and diced
¾ cup plain nonfat yogurt
6 scallions, sliced
1 pickled jalapeño pepper, drained, seeded and minced,
with 1 tablespoon liquid
½ teaspoon dried oregano leaves

In a medium bowl, combine all the ingredients. Refrigerate, covered, until the flavors are blended, at least 1 hour.

Per serving: 56 CALORIES, 0 G TOTAL FAT, 0 G SATURATED FAT, 1 MG CHOLESTEROL, 119 MG SODIUM, 10 G TOTAL CARBOHYDRATE, 2 G DIETARY FIBER, 4 G PROTEIN, 114 MG CALCIUM.

POINTS PER SERVING: 1

Tip

Serve this cool yet zippy condiment with Baby Lamp Chops (page 167). Or try it instead of salsa with baked tortilla chips.

Minted Zucchini

Makes 4 servings

4 teaspoons olive oil
4 medium zucchini, thinly sliced
3 tablespoons finely chopped mint
1 garlic clove, crushed
½ teaspoon salt
¼ teaspoon freshly ground pepper

In a large nonstick skillet, heat 2 teaspoons of the oil. Sauté the zucchini until golden brown, 7–8 minutes (depending on the size of your skillet, you may have to do this in batches). Transfer to a bowl. Add the mint, garlic, salt, pepper and the remaining 2 teaspoons of oil; toss to combine. Refrigerate, covered, until the flavors are blended, about 2 hours.

Per serving: 60 CALORIES, 5 G TOTAL FAT, 1 G SATURATED FAT, 0 MG CHOLESTEROL, 278 MG SODIUM, 4 G TOTAL CARBOHYDRATE, 1 G DIETARY FIBER, 2 G PROTEIN, 25 MG CALCIUM.

POINTS PER SERVING: 1

Tip

To make the most of all your garden's bounty, toss in a few chopped tomatoes when adding the remaining ingredients to the zucchini.

Frozen Yogurt Sundaes

Makes 4 servings

¼ cup walnuts, coarsely chopped (optional)
¼ cup semisweet chocolate chips
1 tablespoon smooth peanut butter
1 tablespoon skim milk
One 16-ounce container nonfat sugar-free frozen yogurt
(chocolate, vanilla or coffee)

1. If you are using the walnuts, toast them to boost their flavor: Line a microwavable plate with a paper towel; place the walnuts in a single layer on the plate. Microwave on High until fragrant, 1–2 minutes.
2. In a 2-cup microwavable bowl, mix the chocolate chips, peanut butter and milk; microwave on Medium (50% power), stirring once, until the chocolate is melted and smooth, 1–2 minutes. Stir in the walnuts.
3. Serve the frozen yogurt, topped with the chocolate sauce.

Per serving (with walnuts): 198 CALORIES, 9 G TOTAL FAT, 2 G SATURATED FAT, 0 MG CHOLESTEROL, 101 MG SODIUM, 24 G TOTAL CARBOHYDRATE, 2 G DIETARY FIBER, 9 G PROTEIN, 161 MG CALCIUM.

POINTS PER SERVING: 4

_____ Tip _____

If you decide not to use the nuts, you'll save 1 **POINT**. And don't get complacent about label-reading when it comes to frozen desserts. Many of these so-called "healthy" or "low-fat" products still pack significant amounts of calories and, yes, even fat. Check the label: a 4-ounce serving that provides 100–150 calories and 2–3 grams of fat is a good baseline.

Sunday Night Supper

Sunday tends to be my favorite day. It is the one day of the week when I can spend the most time with my children, which makes it a very special time. We play games, go riding, or swimming in the summer and for long, long walks. We also make great use of the trampoline in the garden. That trampoline has saved my sanity on more than one occasion! We also just talk and enjoy each other's company, without the office calling me. Dinner is an early, informal event where we can all talk together.

Serves 4

Cider Pork Chops

Ginger Pear and Apple Sauce

Stuffed Sweet Dumpling Squash

Parsley Rice

Angel Food Cake with Lemon Curd

Cider Pork Chops

Makes 4 servings

3 tablespoons all-purpose flour
½ teaspoon freshly ground pepper
¼ teaspoon salt
Four 4-ounce lean boneless center-cut pork loin chops
2 teaspoons vegetable oil
½ cup apple cider
1 tablespoon cider vinegar
1 teaspoon grated lemon zest

1. In a gallon-size sealable plastic bag, combine the flour, ¼ teaspoon of the pepper and the salt; one at a time, add the pork chops and shake to coat.

2. In a large nonstick skillet, heat the oil. Sauté the pork until lightly browned, 1–2 minutes on each side. Reduce the heat and add the cider; simmer, covered, until the pork is cooked through and tender, 15–20 minutes. With a slotted spatula, transfer the pork to a platter; keep warm.

3. Add the vinegar and lemon zest to the pan juices; bring to a boil. Cook, stirring occasionally, until slightly thickened, about 5 minutes; season with the remaining ¼ teaspoon of pepper. Spoon the sauce over the pork.

Per serving: 231 CALORIES, 10 G TOTAL FAT, 3 G SATURATED FAT, 73 MG CHOLESTEROL, 188 MG SODIUM, 8 G TOTAL CARBOHYDRATE, 0 G DIETARY FIBER, 22 G PROTEIN, 10 MG CALCIUM.

POINTS PER SERVING: 5

Tip

The zest of the lemon is the peel without any of the pith (white membrane). To remove the zest from the lemon, use a zester or the fine side of a vegetable grater.

Ginger Pear and Apple Sauce

Makes 4 servings

2 teaspoons vegetable oil
2 shallots, minced
2 teaspoons grated peeled gingerroot
Pinch ground allspice
Pinch salt
Pinch freshly ground pepper
3 pears, peeled, cored and chopped
1 McIntosh apple, peeled, cored and chopped
½ cup apple juice
¼ cup dry white wine
¼ teaspoon grated lemon zest

In a medium nonstick saucepan, heat the oil. Sauté the shallots, gingerroot, allspice, salt and pepper until the shallots are softened, about 3 minutes. Stir in the pears, apple, apple juice, wine and lemon zest; cook, stirring gently, until the fruit is very tender, about 15 minutes.

Per serving: 101 CALORIES, 2 G TOTAL FAT, 0 G SATURATED FAT, 0 MG CHOLESTEROL, 36 MG SODIUM, 19 G TOTAL CARBOHYDRATE, 3 G DIETARY FIBER, 0 G PROTEIN, 11 MG CALCIUM.

POINTS PER SERVING: 2

Tip

Use the ripest pears you can find. Bartletts, Anjous or Boscs will do the trick. McIntosh apples cook down considerably; peeling them eliminates the unpleasant texture. Spoon a pool of this spicy sauce alongside a favorite pork or chicken dish.

Stuffed Sweet Dumpling Squash

Makes 4 servings

Two 1-pound sweet dumpling squash, halved and seeded

2 teaspoons reduced-calorie margarine

1 large onion, diced

2 apples, peeled, cored and diced

1 celery stalk, diced

¼ cup golden raisins

1. Preheat the oven to 350° F. Place the squash, cut-side down, in a 9 x 13" baking dish. Cover with foil and bake 10 minutes.

2. Meanwhile, in a medium nonstick skillet, melt the margarine. Sauté the onion until softened, about 3 minutes. Stir in the apples, celery and raisins; cook, stirring frequently, until the apples are soft, 5–6 minutes. Divide the filling among the squash. Re-cover with the foil and bake until the squash is soft and the filling is lightly browned, about 40 minutes.

Per serving: 140 CALORIES, 1 G TOTAL FAT, 0 G SATURATED FAT, 0 MG CHOLESTEROL, 43 MG SODIUM, 34 G TOTAL CARBOHYDRATE, 8 G DIETARY FIBER, 2 G PROTEIN, 76 MG CALCIUM.

POINTS PER SERVING: 1

Tip

Sweet dumpling squash is rather squat; it has green skin with white stripes. The common acorn, or the less well-known delicata squash (it's shaped somewhat like a cucumber, with green-and-beige striped skin) can be used instead of the sweet dumpling, if you like. Whichever you choose, be sure to select a squash that feels heavy for its size.

Parsley Rice

Makes 4 servings

1 cup long-grain white rice
1 teaspoon vegetable oil
½ celery stalk, minced
1 garlic clove, minced
½ cup minced flat-leaf parsley
¼ teaspoon dried thyme leaves, crumbled

1. Cook the rice according to package directions.
2. In a medium nonstick skillet, heat the oil. Sauté the celery and garlic until they just begin to soften, 1–2 minutes. Stir in the parsley and thyme; cook, stirring constantly, until the vegetables are softened, about 2 minutes longer. Add to the rice; toss to combine.

Per serving: 184 Calories, 2 g Total Fat, 0 g Saturated Fat, 0 mg Cholesterol, 11 mg Sodium, 38 g Total Carbohydrate, 1 g Dietary Fiber, 4 g Protein, 28 mg Calcium.

POINTS PER SERVING: 4

Tip

If you're looking to boost this recipe's nutrient content, stir in 1 cup chopped spinach when you add the parsley and thyme.

Angel Food Cake with Lemon Curd

Makes 16 servings

Lemon Curd

¾ cup granulated sugar

2 tablespoons cornstarch

1 tablespoon grated lemon zest

½ cup lemon juice

2 tablespoons reduced-calorie margarine

2 egg yolks

Cake

1½ cups cake flour

1½ cups granulated sugar

12 egg whites, at room temperature

1½ teaspoons cream of tartar

½ teaspoon salt

2 teaspoons vanilla extract

Confectioners' sugar, for dusting

1. To prepare the lemon curd, in a medium nonstick saucepan, mix the sugar, cornstarch and lemon zest; whisk in the lemon juice, margarine and ½ cup water, stirring until the sugar dissolves. Bring to a boil; cook, stirring constantly, until the mixture thickens slightly, about 1 minute.

2. In a small bowl, lightly beat the egg yolks. Slowly whisk ¼ cup of the lemon mixture into the egg yolks, then slowly pour the egg-yolk mixture into the lemon mixture, whisking quickly and constantly. Reduce the heat to low and cook 1 minute longer; do not let the mixture boil. Transfer the lemon curd to a bowl; refrigerate, covered, until chilled, at least 3 hours.

3. To make the cake, preheat the oven to 375° F. In a sifter or large strainer, combine the flour and ¾ cup of the granulated sugar; sift into a small bowl.

4. In a very large bowl, with an electric mixer on high speed, beat the egg whites, cream of tartar and salt until soft peaks form; add the vanilla. With the mixer at high speed, sprinkle in the remaining ¾ cup sugar, 2 tablespoons at a time, until the sugar completely dissolves and whites stand in stiff peaks. With a rubber spatula, fold the flour mixture into the egg whites just until the flour mixture disappears.

5. Pour the batter into an ungreased 10″ tube pan. Bake until the cake springs back when lightly touched, 35–40 minutes. Invert the cake in the pan onto funnel or bottle; cool completely in the pan.

6. To serve, with a metal spatula, carefully loosen the cake from pan; place on a cake plate, bottom-side up. With a long serrated knife, carefully cut the cake crosswise in half. Spread the cake with the lemon curd, letting some flow down the sides of the cake. Replace the top of the cake. Sprinkle with the confectioners' sugar. Serve at once.

Per serving: 181 CALORIES, 1 G TOTAL FAT, 0 G SATURATED FAT, 27 MG CHOLESTEROL, 126 MG SODIUM, 38 G TOTAL CARBOHYDRATE, 0 G DIETARY FIBER, 4 G PROTEIN, 8 MG CALCIUM.

POINTS PER SERVING: 4

Tip

This lightened version of lemon curd helps to make an impressive dessert; if you're pressed for time, use a store-bought cake. Angel food cake is delicate, so be sure to use a serrated knife with a long blade for easier slicing. Don't be tempted to use egg substitute instead of egg whites—it doesn't whip up.

A Tuscan Dinner

The time of the year that I insist is mine and mine alone is when my children are on summer school holiday. Summer holiday is when we reconnect as a family and I reconnect to myself.

I have just spent the summer in Tuscany with the girls. It truly is one of the most beautiful parts of the world. The small country towns have names I have long recognized on bottles of delicious wines.

A glass of fine wine is something I enjoy with my meal. I have learned that I can have a glass of wine with dinner or a wonderful dessert. But I must tally up everything, and I must watch portions. I now realize overeating is only a symptom of suppressed feelings. When I was at my highest weight, I believe I had truly lost control of my life. I would reach out for food instead of delving deeply into my feelings. Now I know not to go on with life mindlessly; I try to be mindful of every moment—with my children and with myself.

Serves 4

Crock of Italian Olives*

Warm White Bean Salad

Lemon Chicken

Steamed Broccoli*

Spicy Polenta

Bittersweet Fruit

Warm White Bean Salad

Makes 4 servings

4 teaspoons olive oil

4 plum tomatoes, seeded and chopped

1 onion, minced

2 tablespoons minced fresh sage, or 1 teaspoon dried

1 garlic clove, minced

¼ teaspoon salt

¼ teaspoon freshly ground pepper

One 16-ounce can cannellini beans, rinsed and drained

In a medium nonstick skillet, heat the oil. Sauté the tomatoes, onion, sage, garlic, salt and pepper until the sauce thickens, about 5 minutes. Stir in the beans.

Per serving: 138 CALORIES, 5 G TOTAL FAT, 1 G SATURATED FAT, 0 MG CHOLESTEROL, 264 MG SODIUM, 18 G TOTAL CARBOHYDRATE, 6 G DIETARY FIBER, 6 G PROTEIN, 40 MG CALCIUM.

POINTS PER SERVING: 2

Tip

This salad makes an ideal stuffing for peppers: Halve and seed 4 red bell peppers, then bake at 425° F until tender, about 30 minutes; drain any liquid from the peppers before stuffing them.

A Tuscan Dinner

Lemon Chicken

Makes 4 servings

1 tablespoon all-purpose flour

¼ teaspoon salt

¼ teaspoon freshly ground pepper

Four 4-ounce skinless boneless chicken breasts, pounded into ¼" scallops

2 teaspoons olive oil

½ cup chicken broth

2 tablespoons fresh lemon juice

1 tablespoon chopped flat-leaf parsley

1 tablespoon capers, rinsed and drained

Lemon slices, to garnish

1. On a sheet of wax paper, combine the flour, salt and pepper. Coat one side of each chicken scallop with the flour mixture.
2. In a medium nonstick skillet, heat the oil. Add the chicken, floured-side down; cook until lightly browned and cooked through, about 1 minute on each side. Transfer to a plate.
3. In the skillet, mix the broth, lemon juice, parsley and capers; bring to a boil. Cook until the liquid is reduced to about ⅓ cup, about 2 minutes. Return the chicken and any accumulated juices to the skillet; cook until just heated through, 1–2 minutes. Serve, garnished with the lemon slices.

Per serving: 167 Calories, 5 g Total Fat, 1 g Saturated Fat, 71 mg Cholesterol, 365 mg Sodium, 2 g Total Carbohydrate, 0 g Dietary Fiber, 26 g Protein, 16 mg Calcium.

POINTS PER SERVING: 4

This recipe also works with veal or turkey scallops in place of the chicken. To keep raw meat from spattering all over your kitchen when you pound the scallops, place the chicken breasts between sheets of wax paper; if you don't have a meat mallet, use a small skillet.

Spicy Polenta

Makes 4 servings

1 teaspoon salt
1 cup cornmeal
½ teaspoon crushed red pepper flakes, or to taste

1. Spray an 8 x 4" loaf pan with nonstick cooking spray.
2. In a large heavy saucepan, bring 3 cups water and the salt to a boil. Reduce the heat and gradually add the cornmeal in a slow, thin stream, whisking constantly to prevent lumps from forming. Cook, stirring frequently, until thickened, 5–10 minutes. Stir in the pepper flakes. Spread the polenta into the pan, smoothing the top. Refrigerate, covered, until firm, at least 30 minutes.
3. Preheat the oven to 350° F; lightly spray a baking sheet with nonstick cooking spray. Invert the loaf pan to release the polenta, then cut into 1" slices; place on the baking sheet. Bake until the edges are golden brown, about 30 minutes.

Per serving: 158 CALORIES, 1 G TOTAL FAT, 0 G SATURATED FAT, 0 MG CHOLESTEROL, 552 MG SODIUM, 33 G TOTAL CARBOHYDRATE, 2 G DIETARY FIBER, 4 G PROTEIN, 7 MG CALCIUM.

POINTS PER SERVING: 3

Tip

To make this an entrée, stir in ½ cup grated Parmesan cheese with the pepper. Serve with a zesty ratatouille to round out the meal.

Bittersweet Fruit

Makes 4 servings

1 blood orange, peeled and thinly sliced
1 navel orange, peeled and thinly sliced
1 cup honeydew melon chunks
¼ cup Italian bitters

1. Arrange the oranges on a platter.
2. In a small bowl, combine the melon and bitters; spoon over the oranges. Refrigerate, covered, until chilled, at least 30 minutes.

Per serving: 99 Calories, 0 g Total Fat, 0 g Saturated Fat, 0 mg Cholesterol, 1 mg Sodium, 19 g Total Carbohydrate, 2 g Dietary Fiber, 1 g Protein, 32 mg Calcium.

POINTS PER SERVING: 2

Tip

Italian bitters, such as Campari®, are available in most liquor stores. For a refreshing apéritif, serve a dash of bitters in sparkling mineral water with a twist of lemon (bitters have a reputation as an excellent digestive). If blood oranges aren't available, tangerines will do the trick.

A Working Mother's Lunch

Sooner or later, every working mother realizes the importance of having a solid support system in place.

As a young working girl, living in Clapham and before my engagement to Prince Andrew, I subsisted on black coffee and ill-balanced meals. As a result, I became a weak, jittery wreck, completely wired. I used to feel faint in the middle of the day through lack of food.

I was always dieting, at least when I wasn't bingeing.

Thankfully, I have since learned the importance of finding time to eat three balanced meals each day. I have also learned that the road to happiness is not paved with a thin body, and no one need struggle alone when it comes to weight. Now, I turn to my old friends and new Weight Watchers friends to provide support when I need it.

Serves 4

Gorgonzola and Pear Pizza
Arugula and Watercress Salad
Fresh Tangerines*

Gorgonzola and Pear Pizza

Makes 4 servings

½ pound prepared pizza dough
1 teaspoon extra virgin olive oil
1 large pear, thinly sliced
⅓ cup crumbled Gorgonzola cheese

1. Spray the grill rack with nonstick cooking spray; preheat the grill.
2. On a lightly floured surface, divide the dough into fourths; roll out each into rounds ⅛" thick. Carefully place the dough directly onto the grill rack; brush the tops with the oil. Grill until the dough bubbles on the top and begins to char on the bottom, about 2 minutes; turn over. Divide the pear and cheese over the crusts; cover the grill or tent with foil and grill until the cheese melts and crust is crisp, 3–5 minutes.

Per serving: 282 Calories, 6 g Total Fat, 2 g Saturated Fat, 8 mg Cholesterol, 423 mg Sodium, 49 g Total Carbohydrate, 4 g Dietary Fiber, 8 g Protein, 74 mg Calcium.

POINTS PER SERVING: 5

Tip

If you find whole-wheat pizza dough (which gives a crisper crust than white-flour dough), it is ideal with these toppings. Ask for it at your local pizzeria or bakery.

Arugula and Watercress Salad

Makes 4 servings

1½ teaspoons Dijon mustard
1 garlic clove, minced
1½ tablespoons honey
1 tablespoon champagne vinegar
1 bunch watercress, cleaned and coarsely chopped
1 small bunch arugula (about ¼ pound), cleaned and coarsely chopped
1 carrot, shredded

1. In a small bowl, mix the mustard and garlic; whisk in the honey and vinegar.
2. In a large salad bowl, combine the watercress, arugula and carrot. Drizzle with the dressing; toss to coat.

Per serving: 46 CALORIES, 0 G TOTAL FAT, 0 G SATURATED FAT, 0 MG CHOLESTEROL, 37 MG SODIUM, 10 G TOTAL CARBOHYDRATE, 1 G DIETARY FIBER, 2 G PROTEIN, 88 MG CALCIUM.

POINTS PER SERVING: 1

Tip

Remove all of the thick, woody stems when cleaning fresh watercress.

Supper After a Horseback Ride

From an early age, I have loved riding horses. When we moved to Dummer Down, a dairy farm Dads inherited, I was in heaven. Located in the depths of the English countryside in Hampshire, England, Dummer was *real* country: acres of rolling pasture, fields filled with corn, oats and barley, an apple orchard. And the stables: My most vivid memories of Dummer somehow all lead back to riding my treasured horses.

Throughout my childhood, I had a succession of extraordinary horses and ponies who were faithful and always pushed themselves for me. When I was about nine years of age, Herbert, my chestnut pony, was my trusty friend. I remember once he stood stock-still when I got my foot caught in the stirrup. Most little ponies would have run away, but not Herbert.

As an adult, I certainly have been to my fair share of events. However, the most grueling test of my riding ability was the Qatar Horse Marathon on the Arabian Peninsula. The event is commonly known as "Desert Storm," and for good reason: you ride your horse across 26 miles of barren desert. The horse that carried me through was Gal, an Akhal-Teke, a Russian breed that was once favored by the likes of Alexander the Great. Desert Storm truly was a formidable task, but it did show me I can do whatever I put my mind to.

Serves 8

Sun-Dried Tomato and Smoked Mozzarella Crostini
Fennel and Blood Orange Salad with Sweet Onions
Classic Roast Beef with Wild Mushrooms
Haricots Verts
Braised Leeks
Basil-Rice Pilaf
Strawberries in Champagne

Sun-Dried Tomato and Smoked Mozzarella Crostini

Makes 8 servings

16 sun-dried tomatoes (not oil-packed)
2 plum tomatoes, chopped
2 tablespoons low-sodium tomato juice
4 teaspoons olive oil
2 garlic cloves, minced
Sixteen ½″ slices crusty Italian bread, toasted
⅔ cup shredded smoked mozzarella cheese
½ teaspoon dried thyme leaves, crumbled
½ teaspoon dried oregano, crumbled

1. Line the broiler pan with foil, shiny-side up; preheat the broiler.
2. In a food processor or blender, combine the sun-dried tomatoes, plum tomatoes, tomato juice, oil and garlic; puree. Spread about 1 teaspoon of the tomato mixture on each slice of toast, then sprinkle with the mozzarella, thyme and oregano. Broil 1 minute, until the cheese is melted and bubbling. Serve at once.

Per serving: 133 CALORIES, 5 G TOTAL FAT, 2 G SATURATED FAT, 7 MG CHOLESTEROL, 317 MG SODIUM, 18 G TOTAL CARBOHYDRATE, 2 G DIETARY FIBER, 7 G PROTEIN, 102 MG CALCIUM.

POINTS PER SERVING: 3

Tip

If you're not a fan of smoked flavors, just use the plain mozzarella—but do make the effort to find fresh, sold in balls in some supermarkets, gourmet stores and Italian delis. Smoked mozzarella is seldom available in any but the whole-milk version. Using skim-milk mozzarella will save you 1 *POINT*.

A Working Mother's Lunch

GORGONZOLA AND PEAR PIZZA

Supper After a Horseback Ride

CLASSIC ROAST BEEF WITH WILD MUSHROOMS

A Perfect Picnic

SPINACH CHICKEN SALAD, TOMATO PARMESAN TOASTS

A Girlfriends' Get-Together

BEET AND APPLE "NAPOLEON"

An American Barbecue

BARBECUE BEEF SANDWICH, RAINBOW COLE SLAW,
ROASTED CORN ON THE COB WITH CILANTRO BUTTER, ICED TEA

Afternoon Tea

Top: OPEN-FACE HAM SANDWICHES AND CUCUMBER SANDWICHES
Middle: ALMOND BISCOTTI AND CHOCOLATE MOUSSE TARTLETS
Bottom: PEAR-PORT QUICK BREAD AND BLACKBERRY SCONES

Afternoon Tea

ALMOND BISCOTTI, BLACKBERRY SCONES,
CHOCOLATE MOUSSE TARTLET

A Provençal Feast

MEDITERRANEAN FISHERMAN'S STEW, CRUSTY BAGUETTE

Fennel and Blood Orange Salad with Sweet Onions

Makes 8 servings

¼ cup red-wine vinegar

¼ cup orange juice

4 teaspoons sugar

4 teaspoons olive oil

1 teaspoon Dijon mustard

¼ teaspoon salt

Freshly ground pepper, to taste

2 large fennel bulbs

4 large blood oranges, peeled and cut into ¼″ slices

2 sweet onions, cut into ⅛″ slices and separated into rings

1. In a small bowl, whisk the vinegar, orange juice, sugar, oil, mustard, salt and pepper.
2. Cut the feathery tops and stems from the fennel bulb and discard. Trim any yellow or bruised outer leaves, then cut the bulb in half through the stem end. Cut out the tough core; place the halves, cut-side down, on a cutting board. With a sharp knife, cut the fennel crosswise into paper-thin slices. Divide the slices among 8 salad plates; top with the orange slices and onion rings. Drizzle with the dressing.

Per serving: 130 CALORIES, 3 G TOTAL FAT, 0 G SATURATED FAT, 0 MG CHOLESTEROL, 126 MG SODIUM, 26 G TOTAL CARBOHYDRATE, 2 G DIETARY FIBER, 3 G PROTEIN, 119 MG CALCIUM.

POINTS PER SERVING: 2

Tip

Feel free to substitute navel oranges or tangerines for the blood oranges.

Classic Roast Beef with Wild Mushrooms

Makes 8 servings

One 2-pound eye round beef roast
½ teaspoon salt
½ teaspoon freshly ground pepper
2 teaspoons olive oil
1 onion, diced
1 cup chopped shiitake mushrooms
1 cup chopped cremini mushrooms
½ cup chopped porcini mushrooms
1 garlic clove, minced
¼ cup red wine
1 tablespoon minced parsley
½ teaspoon dried thyme leaves, crumbled

1. Preheat the oven to 325° F; spray a rack with nonstick cooking spray and place in a large roasting pan. Season the beef with the salt and pepper; place on the rack. Roast until the beef reaches an internal temperature of 145–150° F, about 1 hour. Transfer to a cutting board and let stand 10–15 minutes.

2. Meanwhile, in a medium nonstick skillet, heat the oil. Sauté the onion until softened, about 3 minutes. Add all three kinds of mushrooms and the garlic; sauté, stirring constantly, 5 minutes longer. Stir in the wine, parsley and thyme; cook, stirring constantly, until the mushrooms are soft, 5–6 minutes. Slice the beef and serve with the mushrooms on the side.

Per serving: 171 CALORIES, 5 G TOTAL FAT, 2 G SATURATED FAT, 59 MG CHOLESTEROL, 188 MG SODIUM, 3 G TOTAL CARBOHYDRATE, 1 G DIETARY FIBER, 25 G PROTEIN, 14 MG CALCIUM.

POINTS PER SERVING: 4

Tip

If there are any leftovers, slice up the cold roast for next-day sandwiches. Top with a bit of the remaining mushrooms and a dollop of zesty horseradish for a satisfying lunch. If you have trouble finding fresh porcinis, use dried: Soak ¼ cup in hot water until pliable, about 20 minutes. Add the mushrooms and the soaking liquid with the wine and herbs; there's no need to strain them.

Haricots Verts

Makes 8 servings

2 teaspoons olive oil
4 garlic cloves, minced
4 cups fresh haricots verts
¼ teaspoon salt

In a medium nonstick skillet, heat the oil. Sauté the garlic until golden brown, 1–2 minutes. Stir in the haricots, salt and 3 tablespoons water; cook, covered, until the haricots are tender, about 2 minutes.

Per serving: 48 Calories, 1 g Total Fat, 0 g Saturated Fat, 0 mg Cholesterol, 41 mg Sodium, 9 g Total Carbohydrate, 2 g Dietary Fiber, 2 g Protein, 37 mg Calcium.

POINTS PER SERVING: 1

Tip

The slender French green beans called haricots verts (pronounced *ah-ree-co vair*) are a delicacy. If they are unavailable at your market, use the smallest fresh green beans you can find; increase the cooking time to about 5 minutes.

Braised Leeks

Makes 8 servings

8 medium leeks, halved lengthwise and cleaned
½ cup chicken broth
¼ cup minced parsley
¼ cup white-wine vinegar
2 tablespoons olive oil
1 teaspoon minced thyme leaves
1 teaspoon grated orange zest
1 teaspoon Dijon mustard
½ teaspoon salt
¼ teaspoon freshly ground pepper

1. Preheat the oven to 350° F. In a 9 x 13" baking dish, combine the leeks and broth. Cover with foil and bake until tender, about 25 minutes.
2. Meanwhile, in a small bowl, combine the parsley, vinegar, oil, thyme, orange zest, mustard, salt and pepper with 2 teaspoons water. Serve the leeks, drizzled with the vinaigrette.

Per serving: 93 CALORIES, 4 G TOTAL FAT, 0 G SATURATED FAT, 0 MG CHOLESTEROL, 171 MG SODIUM, 15 G TOTAL CARBOHYDRATE, 1 G DIETARY FIBER, 2 G PROTEIN, 64 MG CALCIUM.

POINTS PER SERVING: 2

Tip

Leeks, with their subtle flavor, make an excellent side dish for grilled fish or chicken, like Baked Chicken with Wine (page 20) or Citrus Red Snapper (page 87).

Basil-Rice Pilaf

Makes 8 servings

4 teaspoons olive oil
1 red bell pepper, seeded and minced
6 scallions, sliced
1½ cups regular (not converted) long-grain rice
12 large black olives, pitted and chopped
1 teaspoon salt
¼ teaspoon cayenne pepper, or to taste
½ cup chopped basil

1. In a large nonstick saucepan, heat the oil. Sauté the bell pepper and scallions until they just begin to soften, 4–5 minutes. Stir in the rice and olives; cook, stirring constantly, until the vegetables are softened and the rice becomes opaque, 2–3 minutes longer.
2. Stir in the salt, cayenne and 3 cups water; bring to a boil. Reduce the heat and simmer, covered, until the liquid is absorbed, 15–20 minutes. Fluff with a fork; re-cover and let stand 5 minutes, then stir in the basil.

Per serving: 163 CALORIES, 3 G TOTAL FAT, 0 G SATURATED FAT, 0 MG CHOLESTEROL, 328 MG SODIUM, 30 G TOTAL CARBOHYDRATE, 1 G DIETARY FIBER, 3 G PROTEIN, 26 MG CALCIUM.

POINTS PER SERVING: 3

Tip

We like the flavor of basil in this dish, but herbs like oregano or parsley or greens like spinach or watercress would be tasty as well. Take your inspiration from whatever looks best in your garden or at the farm stand.

Strawberries in Champagne

Makes 8 servings

24 small whole strawberries
4 cups champagne, chilled

Place 3 strawberries in each of 8 champagne flutes; top with the champagne.

Per serving: 103 CALORIES, 0 G TOTAL FAT, 0 G SATURATED FAT, 0 MG CHOLESTEROL,
7 MG SODIUM, 6 G TOTAL CARBOHYDRATE, 2 G DIETARY FIBER, 1 G PROTEIN,
21 MG CALCIUM.

POINTS PER SERVING: 2

Tip

Look for long-stemmed strawberries; leave the stems on the whole berries for easy plucking from your champagne flute.

A Casual Weeknight Supper

Without question, losing weight is *hard*. At least it has been for me. Despite all my years of losing, then more often than not, regaining the weight, I never truly understood the *how* of losing weight. I did the mad crash diets—like the one when I lived on meat and oranges so that I could lose 26 pounds to fit into my wedding gown! But now I truly understand all the hard work that goes into losing weight—and trying to keep it off.

I work every single day at staying healthy and trim. It certainly is one of the greatest challenges I have ever encountered. But now that I am a mother—a mother who wants to set a good example for her daughters—I know that living a healthy, happy life is a priority.

Serves 4

Chicken Calvados

Oven-Roasted Root Vegetables

Peppered Parsley Noodles

Parmesan-Baked Asparagus

Chicken Calvados

Makes 4 servings

½ teaspoon salt
½ teaspoon freshly ground pepper
¼ teaspoon cinnamon
¼ teaspoon ground ginger
Four 4-ounce skinless boneless chicken breasts
4 teaspoons vegetable oil
2 onions, thinly sliced
4 Golden Delicious apples, peeled, cored and thinly sliced
1 cup apple cider or apple juice
2 tablespoons Calvados (apple brandy)

1. In a small bowl, combine the salt, pepper, cinnamon and ginger. Rub into the chicken.
2. In a large nonstick skillet, heat the oil. Sauté the chicken until browned, about 3 minutes on each side. Transfer to a plate.
3. In the skillet, sauté the onions until softened, about 5 minutes. Stir in the apples and cook, turning occasionally, until golden brown and tender, 3–5 minutes. Stir in the cider; bring to a boil. Return the chicken to the skillet and cook, turning as needed, until cooked through, about 5 minutes longer. Transfer to a platter.
4. Stir the Calvados into the skillet; cook until the apples and onions are glazed and the liquid is thickened, about 3 minutes. Serve the chicken, topped with the apple mixture.

Per serving: 286 CALORIES, 6 G TOTAL FAT, 1 G SATURATED FAT, 66 MG CHOLESTEROL, 350 MG SODIUM, 28 G TOTAL CARBOHYDRATE, 3 G DIETARY FIBER, 27 G PROTEIN, 33 MG CALCIUM.

POINTS PER SERVING: 6

Continued on next page.

Calvados, a French apple brandy produced in Normandy, is distilled from cider, much in the same way that cognac and armagnac are distilled from wine. Its flavor marries well with pork dishes, too. If you prefer, use apple jack or plain brandy.

Oven-Roasted Root Vegetables

Makes 4 servings

1 tablespoon olive oil

¾ pound new potatoes, scrubbed

1 large sweet potato, peeled and cut into chunks

4 carrots, scrubbed and cut into chunks

2 parsnips, peeled and cut into chunks

2 onions, cut into chunks

½ cup chicken broth

2 garlic cloves, minced

½ teaspoon dried thyme leaves, crumbled

½ teaspoon salt

¼ teaspoon freshly ground pepper

1. Preheat the oven to 400° F. Place the oil in a large shallow roasting pan. Heat the oil in the oven until hot, about 5 minutes. Add the new potatoes, sweet potato, carrots, parsnips and onions.
2. In a small bowl, combine the broth, garlic, thyme, salt and pepper. Pour over the vegetables; toss to coat. Roast the vegetables, stirring as needed, until tender, about 45 minutes.

Per serving: 279 CALORIES, 4 G TOTAL FAT, 0 G SATURATED FAT, 0 MG CHOLESTEROL, 490 MG SODIUM, 57 G TOTAL CARBOHYDRATE, 9 G DIETARY FIBER, 6 G PROTEIN, 81 MG CALCIUM.

POINTS PER SERVING: 4

Tip

Roast vegetables are an easy accompaniment to almost any meat or poultry dish—use this combination, or whatever strikes your fancy. Just be sure they're not crowded into the pan when they're roasting.

Peppered Parsley Noodles

Makes 4 servings

1½ cups medium egg noodles
½ cup minced flat-leaf parsley
½ teaspoon cracked black pepper
¼ teaspoon salt

1. Cook the noodles according to package directions; drain, reserving ¼ cup of the cooking liquid, and place in a medium bowl.
2. Add the cooking liquid, parsley, pepper and salt to the noodles; toss to combine.

Per serving: 58 CALORIES, 1 G TOTAL FAT, 0 G SATURATED FAT, 14 MG CHOLESTEROL, 141 MG SODIUM, 11 G TOTAL CARBOHYDRATE, 0 G DIETARY FIBER, 2 G PROTEIN, 17 MG CALCIUM.

POINTS PER SERVING: 1

Tip

Of the more than 30 different kinds of parsley, the two most common are curly (the pretty sprigs of which are often used as garnishes) and the more flavorful flat-leaf (sometimes called Italian) parsley. In dishes such as this, where this herb is given a featured role, you'll want to use flat-leaf parsley.

Parmesan-Baked Asparagus

Makes 4 servings

1 pound asparagus
2 teaspoons olive oil
¼ teaspoon salt
¼ teaspoon freshly ground pepper
¼ cup grated Parmesan cheese

Preheat the oven to 425° F. Place the asparagus on a nonstick baking sheet. Drizzle with the olive oil and sprinkle with the salt and pepper; toss to coat. Bake 10 minutes, then toss again; sprinkle with the cheese and bake until the cheese melts, about 5 minutes longer.

Per serving: 67 CALORIES, 4 G TOTAL FAT, 1 G SATURATED FAT, 4 MG CHOLESTEROL, 237 MG SODIUM, 4 G TOTAL CARBOHYDRATE, 2 G DIETARY FIBER, 5 G PROTEIN, 90 MG CALCIUM.

POINTS PER SERVING: 1

Tip

We like the thinner asparagus spears—unlike their thicker counterparts, they don't need to be peeled. Whichever you use, select a bunch where all the spears are of fairly equal thickness. Baby artichokes, found in better supermarkets, are about the size of walnuts and can be eaten whole—including the leaves. They'd make a novel substitution.

Holiday Buffet

Who doesn't love the holidays? Good cheer, family, friends, great food. For the past few years, the girls and I have spent Christmas at Wood Farm, a lovely farmhouse on the Sandringham Estate where the Royal Family spends the festive season. We have a house full of decorations, and a huge tree, which all help the spirit of the holiday fill every room. We generally have a wonderful feast with everyone taking their place at the table.

The holidays can be a terror if you are trying to lose weight, with sweets and treats at every turn, ready to set you off on a binge. I try not to do that. I find Christmas to be a very quiet and relaxing time. It is a time when I can reflect on the past year's trials and tribulations, as well as its rewards. I have a good deal to be thankful for: two wonderful daughters, good health and a full life.

Serves 12

Mediterranean Tian

Provençal Beef Tenderloin

Turkey Breast with Cremini Mushrooms and Leeks

Risotto di Pavia

Venetian Radicchio

Assorted Breads*

Blueberry Zabaglione

Mediterranean Tian

Makes 12 servings

3 tablespoons olive oil

6 red bell peppers, seeded and quartered

3 medium (about 1¼-pound each) eggplants, thinly sliced

12 scallions, trimmed

¼ cup + 2 tablespoons red-wine vinegar

½ teaspoon dried oregano, crumbled

½ teaspoon dried basil, crumbled

½ teaspoon salt

Freshly ground pepper, to taste

1. Line a baking sheet with foil and spray with nonstick cooking spray; preheat the broiler. Using 1 tablespoon of the oil, brush the peppers, eggplants and scallions on both sides; place on the baking sheet. Broil until slightly charred and fork-tender, about 5 minutes on each side for the peppers, 2–3 minutes on each side for the eggplant, and 1–2 minutes on each side for the scallions. Cut the scallions into 2″ lengths.

2. In a medium bowl, whisk the remaining 2 tablespoons of oil, the vinegar, oregano, basil, salt and pepper with 3 tablespoons water.

3. In two or three shallow serving dishes, alternate layers of the eggplant, peppers and scallions, drizzling a small amount of the vinaigrette over each layer. Pour the remaining dressing over the tops. Refrigerate, covered, until chilled and the flavors are blended, at least 1 hour. Serve at room temperature or slightly chilled.

Per serving: 81 CALORIES, 4 G TOTAL FAT, 0 G SATURATED FAT, 0 MG CHOLESTEROL, 41 MG SODIUM, 12 G TOTAL CARBOHYDRATE, 3 G DIETARY FIBER, 2 G PROTEIN, 62 MG CALCIUM.

POINTS PER SERVING: 1

Continued on next page.

A tian (pronounced *tee-yahn*) simply involves alternating layers of vegetables in a shallow dish. This surprisingly easy recipe makes an attractive, brightly colored presentation.

Provençal Beef Tenderloin

Makes 12 servings

One 3-pound beef tenderloin
¾ cup minced parsley
3 tablespoons minced rosemary
3 tablespoons Dijon mustard
6–8 garlic cloves, minced
1 tablespoon minced oregano
1 tablespoon minced thyme
1 tablespoon olive oil
1 teaspoon freshly ground pepper

1. Place the beef on a sheet of plastic wrap. In a small bowl, mix the remaining ingredients to make a paste. Rub the paste all over the beef; wrap in the plastic and refrigerate 1 hour.

2. Meanwhile, preheat the oven to 425° F. Place the beef in a 9 x 13″ baking dish or shallow roasting pan. Roast until the beef reaches an internal temperature of 145° F, about 45 minutes. Transfer to a cutting board and let stand 10 minutes before slicing.

Per serving: 198 CALORIES, 10 G TOTAL FAT, 3 G SATURATED FAT, 71 MG CHOLESTEROL, 146 MG SODIUM, 1 G TOTAL CARBOHYDRATE, 0 G DIETARY FIBER, 24 G PROTEIN, 19 MG CALCIUM.

POINTS PER SERVING: 5

Tip

Take care not to overcook the beef tenderloin. We like to test for doneness with an instant-read thermometer—it's virtually foolproof. The heat-reading element of an instant-read is halfway between the tip of the thermometer and the small indentation that's about 2″ from the tip; to get an accurate reading, make sure the thermometer is deep enough in the meat and that it's not touching bone or fat.

Turkey Breast with Cremini Mushrooms and Leeks

Makes 12 servings

2 tablespoons olive oil

3–4 leeks, cleaned and thinly sliced

1 onion, chopped

4 garlic cloves, minced

2 cups sliced cremini mushrooms

2 teaspoons minced thyme leaves

1 teaspoon salt

1 teaspoon freshly ground pepper

5 slices firm white bread, cubed

¾ cup chicken broth

½ cup flat-leaf parsley, finely chopped

One 3-pound skinless boneless turkey breast

1. Preheat the oven to 350° F. In a large nonstick skillet, heat 1 tablespoon of the oil. Sauté the leeks, onion and garlic until the leeks just begin to soften, 5–7 minutes. Transfer to a large bowl.

2. In the skillet, heat the remaining tablespoon of oil. Sauté the mushrooms with the thyme, ½ teaspoon of the salt and ½ teaspoon of the pepper until the mushrooms are browned and tender, about 10 minutes. Transfer to the bowl; stir in the bread, broth and parsley.

3. Place the turkey, skinned-side down, between two sheets of wax paper. With a meat mallet or small heavy skillet, pound the turkey so it is ½" thick. Transfer to a work surface; spread with the stuffing to within 1" of the edges. Roll up the turkey and tie with kitchen twine; place, seam-side down, on a rack in a roasting pan, then sprinkle with the remaining salt and pepper. Roast, basting occasionally with the pan juices, until the turkey is cooked through,

1¼–1 ½ hours. Transfer to a cutting board and let stand 10 minutes before slicing. Serve with the pan juices on the side.

Per serving: 203 CALORIES, 4 G TOTAL FAT, 1 G SATURATED FAT, 70 MG CHOLESTEROL, 292 MG SODIUM, 12 G TOTAL CARBOHYDRATE, 1 G DIETARY FIBER, 30 G PROTEIN, 56 MG CALCIUM.

POINTS PER SERVING: 4

—— *Tip* ——

Be sure to use only the white and palest-green parts of the leeks, and to wash them thoroughly to remove all traces of grit (leeks grow in sandy soil). If you like, substitute shiitake mushrooms for the cremini.

Risotto di Pavia

Makes 12 servings

12 cups vegetable or chicken broth
1 tablespoon olive oil
2 onions, chopped
4 shallots, chopped
3 cups Arborio rice
¾ cup dry sherry
3 pounds asparagus, cut into 1″ lengths
1½ cups grated Parmesan cheese
1 teaspoon freshly ground pepper

1. In a large saucepan, bring the broth to a boil. Reduce the heat and simmer.
2. In a large nonstick saucepan or Dutch oven, heat the oil. Sauté the onions and shallots until softened, 5–8 minutes. Add the rice; cook, stirring to coat, 1–2 minutes.
3. Add about 1 cup of the broth and the sherry; cook, stirring constantly, until the liquid is absorbed. Continue adding the broth, about 1 cup at a time, stirring while the broth is absorbed, until the rice is just tender; add the asparagus with the last cup of broth. The total cooking time should be about 25–30 minutes. Remove from the heat and stir in the cheese and pepper.

Per serving: 317 CALORIES, 5 G TOTAL FAT, 2 G SATURATED FAT, 8 MG CHOLESTEROL, 285 MG SODIUM, 54 G TOTAL CARBOHYDRATE, 4 G DIETARY FIBER, 11 G PROTEIN, 172 MG CALCIUM.

POINTS PER SERVING: 6

Tip

Because risotto-making is so labor intensive, even if you aren't serving 12, you might want to make a batch this large. It reheats nicely in the microwave, or, for sublime risotto pancakes, mix leftovers with just enough beaten egg to hold the risotto together without making it too moist, then fold in a bit of shredded part-skim mozzarella. Heat a teaspoon or so of oil in a nonstick skillet and drop the risotto mixture into the pan by generous tablespoonfuls, flattening the blobs with the back of the spoon. Cook until golden brown, about 5 minutes on each side.

Venetian Radicchio

Makes 12 servings

3 heads radicchio, cleaned and quartered
¼ cup + 2 tablespoons fresh lemon juice
3 tablespoons olive oil
Pinch freshly ground black pepper

1. In a large nonreactive bowl, combine all the ingredients, tossing to coat. Cover and let stand 1–4 hours, tossing occasionally.
2. Preheat the oven to 425° F. Transfer the radicchio to a baking sheet and roast until just wilted, about 3 minutes on each side. Serve, drizzled with any remaining marinade.

Per serving: 47 CALORIES, 3 G TOTAL FAT, 0 G SATURATED FAT, 0 MG CHOLESTEROL, 9 MG SODIUM, 4 G TOTAL CARBOHYDRATE, 2 G DIETARY FIBER, 1 G PROTEIN, 1 MG CALCIUM.

POINTS PER SERVING: 1

Tip

Fresh radicchio is plentiful in Veneto, a farmland-rich and fertile region of Italy. You've probably seen it in salad blends, but it's also delicious cooked. Besides roasting it, you can toss radicchio on the grill for a few minutes; just be careful not to char the delicate leaves.

Blueberry Zabaglione

Makes 12 servings

6 cups fat-free egg substitute
3 cups skim milk
¾ cup sugar
¼ cup cornstarch
1½ cups dry marsala wine
6 cups blueberries

1. Pour the egg substitute into a large bowl. In a large nonstick saucepan, whisk the milk, sugar and cornstarch, whisking until the sugar dissolves. Bring to a simmer over medium heat, whisking constantly, then cook, whisking constantly, until thickened, 5–6 minutes.
2. Slowly whisk the milk mixture into the egg substitute, then slowly pour back into the saucepan, whisking quickly and constantly. Reduce the heat to low and cook, whisking constantly, until hot, thick and fluffy, 7–10 minutes; do not let the mixture boil. Slowly whisk in the marsala; cook, whisking constantly, 1 minute longer. Serve the zabaglione in wine or parfait glasses, topped with the blueberries.

Per serving: 201 CALORIES, 0 G TOTAL FAT, 0 G SATURATED FAT, 1 MG CHOLESTEROL, 238 MG SODIUM, 30 G TOTAL CARBOHYDRATE, 2 G DIETARY FIBER, 15 G PROTEIN, 123 MG CALCIUM.

POINTS PER SERVING: 4

Tip

Always wash fresh fruit thoroughly to help eliminate troublesome bacteria. Cooking fruit eliminates most potential health risks, but it also lowers the nutrient levels.

Traveler's Repast

Between my charity work and my travels for Weight Watchers, I spend a good deal of my time in transit. I have visited many states in America and have countless fond memories of each one. But I do find it difficult to compare and contrast the states because each one is so individual and distinctive in its own way.

Oklahoma City does hold a special place in my heart, however: I visited the city just after the bombing in 1995 and, like the rest of the world, was devastated by what I saw. I have been back several times and recently revisited the area. Through one of my charities, Chances for Children, I was able to raise money that was donated for building a new pediatric center.

While I recognize that I am quite fortunate to be able to travel the globe, there truly is no place like home. When I do get back from a trip, I most look forward to seeing my girls and sitting down with them. Frankly, after I've been on a long trip, food is not one of my major concerns. But since a traveler's fare is often not the healthiest, I try to reinstate the healthy habits I have learned. I do look forward to a simple, home-cooked meal: some meat, ham or fish, a baked potato and a salad.

Serves 4

Citrus Red Snapper
Baked Potato*
Crunchy Fennel Salad
Pears with Peppered Goat Cheese
Pot of Herbal Tea*

Citrus Red Snapper

Makes 4 servings

2 tablespoons all-purpose flour

¾ teaspoon ground coriander

¾ teaspoon ground ginger

¼ teaspoon cayenne pepper

Four 8-ounce red snapper fillets

2 teaspoons vegetable oil

1 yellow bell pepper, seeded and sliced

3 scallions, sliced

¼ cup low-sodium chicken broth

2 tablespoons orange juice

1 tablespoon fresh lemon juice

1 tablespoon fresh lime juice

Lemon and lime slices, to garnish

1. On a sheet of wax paper, combine the flour, coriander, ginger and cayenne. Coat one side of each fillet with the flour mixture.
2. In a large nonstick skillet, heat the oil. Add the fillets, floured-side down; cook until browned on the bottom, 2–3 minutes. Transfer to a plate.
3. In the skillet, mix the bell pepper, scallions, broth, orange juice, lemon juice and lime juice; return the fish to the skillet, browned-side up. Reduce the heat and cook, covered, until the fish is just opaque and the bell pepper is softened, 3–5 minutes. With a slotted spatula, transfer the fish and vegetables to a platter. Cook the pan juices until they are reduced to about ¼ cup; pour over the fish. Serve, garnished with the lemon and lime slices.

Continued on next page.

Per serving: 279 Calories, 5 g Total Fat, 1 g Saturated Fat, 84 mg Cholesterol, 150 mg Sodium, 7 g Total Carbohydrate, 1 g Dietary Fiber, 48 g Protein, 83 mg Calcium.

POINTS PER SERVING: 6

—— *Tip* ——

Just about any firm-fleshed fish fillets will do the trick in this recipe: Try ocean perch, flounder, sea bass, cod or haddock.

Crunchy Fennel Salad

Makes 4 servings

3 tablespoons white-wine vinegar
2 tablespoons fresh lime juice
1 teaspoon sugar
2 fennel bulbs, trimmed and thinly sliced
½ red onion, thinly sliced

1. In a small bowl, mix the vinegar, lime juice and sugar, stirring until the sugar dissolves.
2. In a large bowl, combine the fennel and onion. Drizzle with the dressing; toss to coat.

Per serving: 31 CALORIES, 0 G TOTAL FAT, 0 G SATURATED FAT, 0 MG CHOLESTEROL, 111 MG SODIUM, 6 G TOTAL CARBOHYDRATE, 1 G DIETARY FIBER, 2 G PROTEIN, 57 MG CALCIUM.

POINTS PER SERVING: 0

Tip

With its subtle licoricelike flavor, fennel (also called anise or *finocchio*) makes a light side dish for a robust, rich entrée like beef or pork. Try it as the Italians do, sliced and unadorned, after dinner as a digestive. (See Step 2 of the Fennel and Blood Orange Salad on page 63 for fennel-trimming instructions.)

Pears with Peppered Goat Cheese

Makes 4 servings

2 large Bosc pears, halved and cored
1 teaspoon fresh lemon juice
⅓ cup crumbled peppered goat cheese

Brush the cut side of the pears with the lemon juice; place the pears on dessert plates. Sprinkle with the cheese.

Per serving: 131 CALORIES, 4 G TOTAL FAT, 2 G SATURATED FAT, 8 MG CHOLESTEROL, 148 MG SODIUM, 24 G TOTAL CARBOHYDRATE, 4 G DIETARY FIBER, 3 G PROTEIN, 74 MG CALCIUM.

POINTS PER SERVING: 2

Tip

Use the ripest pears you can find for this easy yet elegant dessert—their sweetness will provide the most contrast to the tangy bite of the cheese. Experiment with other cheeses; a blue like Roquefort or Gorgonzola would be good. For best flavor, let the cheese come to room temperature.

Gardener's Supper

In my life, a "day off" is almost unheard of; however, if I can catch a few hours of free time, I like to indulge my love of painting.

In a funny way, my painting has helped me on the dieting front. In searching for ways other than eating to indulge my senses, I have happily become reacquainted with my creative side. I enjoy sketching and painting, primarily watercolors.

Nature plays a tremendous role in my work: I use the garden, the mountains, the wilds of Scotland and the beautiful English countryside for inspiration. (I do understand why so many Americans have fallen in love with our English gardens: they are spectacular!)

Thanks to my new habits, I have also discovered the riches of the garden: just-picked produce like wonderfully ripe tomatoes or fresh green beans. I try to include as many fresh vegetables and fruits as possible in all my meals—but never just steamed! Pairing those treasures with small tastes of other foods with intense flavor, like prosciutto or Parmesan, truly can make a simple meal a feast.

Serves 4

Twenty-Minute Minestrone

Stuffed Baby Eggplant

Lemon Couscous

Asparagus Vinaigrette with Parmesan and Prosciutto

Raspberries with Citrus Sauce

Twenty-Minute Minestrone

Makes 4 servings

1 tablespoon olive oil
1 tomato, chopped
1 onion, chopped
1 garlic clove, minced
4 cups chicken broth
2 medium red potatoes, scrubbed and diced
½ pound green beans, cut into 1" lengths
1 medium zucchini, chopped
1 medium yellow squash, chopped
2 cups coarsely chopped cleaned spinach
One 15-ounce can red kidney beans, rinsed and drained
2 tablespoons grated Parmesan cheese

1. In a large nonstick saucepan or Dutch oven, heat the oil. Sauté the tomato, onion and garlic until softened, about 5 minutes. Stir in the broth and potatoes; bring to a boil. Reduce the heat and simmer, partially covered, until the potatoes are almost tender, about 10 minutes.
2. Add the green beans, zucchini and yellow squash; cook until tender, about 5 minutes. Stir in the spinach and kidney beans; cook until heated through, about 3 minutes. Serve, sprinkled with the cheese.

Per serving: 254 Calories, 7 g Total Fat, 2 g Saturated Fat, 19 mg Cholesterol, 1,176 mg Sodium, 39 g Total Carbohydrate, 10 g Dietary Fiber, 12 g Protein, 127 mg Calcium.

POINTS PER SERVING: 4

◆

―――― *Tip* ――――

When the weather starts to cool off, you can make this soup more of a hearty stew by adding small tubular pasta and winter vegetables. Serve it with a crisp Italian white wine like Pinot Grigio and crusty Italian bread.

Stuffed Baby Eggplant

Makes 4 servings

2 baby eggplants, halved lengthwise

1 teaspoon olive oil

1 onion, chopped

1 tomato, diced

1 garlic clove, minced

¼ cup + 2 tablespoons seasoned dried bread crumbs

1 egg, slightly beaten

2 tablespoons grated Parmesan cheese

6 kalamata olives, pitted and chopped

1 tablespoon pine nuts, coarsely chopped and toasted (optional)

1 tablespoon chopped basil

1 tablespoon capers, rinsed, drained and coarsely chopped

1. Preheat the oven to 400° F; spray a shallow 1-quart baking dish with non-stick cooking spray.
2. Fill a medium skillet ½″ deep with water; add the eggplant, cut-side down. Bring to a boil, then reduce the heat and simmer, covered, until the eggplant is fork-tender, about 5 minutes. Drain the eggplant on paper towels.
3. In a small nonstick skillet, heat the oil. Sauté the onion until softened, about 5 minutes. Add the tomato and garlic; cook, stirring occasionally, until the vegetables begin to soften, about 5 minutes. Remove from the heat.
4. With a spoon, carefully scoop out the pulp from each eggplant half, leaving a ¼″ shell. Coarsely chop the pulp.
5. In a medium bowl, mix the eggplant pulp with the sautéed vegetables, the bread crumbs, egg, cheese, olives, pine nuts (if using), basil and capers. Spoon the filling into the eggplant shells and place in the baking dish. Bake until the filling is hot and browned on top, about 25 minutes.

Per serving (with pine nuts): 150 CALORIES, 6 G TOTAL FAT, 1 G SATURATED FAT, 55 MG CHOLESTEROL, 444 MG SODIUM, 20 G TOTAL CARBOHYDRATE, 4 G DIETARY FIBER, 7 G PROTEIN, 76 MG CALCIUM.

POINTS PER SERVING: 3

Tip

Pine nuts, also called pignoli, really are the seeds of a pine cone. They have a mild delicate flavor and are used in many Mediterranean dishes. Pine nuts are highly perishable because of their high fat content; never buy more than you need, and keep them in the refrigerator or freezer (bring them to room temperature before using). Chopped walnuts may be substituted, if you like. Using this small an amount of nuts doesn't affect the *POINTS* per serving.

Lemon Couscous

Makes 4 servings

1¾ cups chicken broth
2 teaspoons grated lemon zest
2 tablespoons fresh lemon juice
1 tablespoon unsalted butter or margarine
¼ teaspoon salt
One 10-ounce box couscous
1 tablespoon chopped parsley

In a medium saucepan, combine the broth, lemon zest, lemon juice, butter and salt; bring to a boil. Stir in the couscous and parsley; cover and remove from the heat. Let stand until the liquid is absorbed, about 5 minutes. Fluff the couscous with a fork.

Per serving: 309 CALORIES, 4 G TOTAL FAT, 2 G SATURATED FAT, 16 MG CHOLESTEROL, 575 MG SODIUM, 56 G TOTAL CARBOHYDRATE, 4 G DIETARY FIBER, 10 G PROTEIN, 22 MG CALCIUM.

POINTS PER SERVING: 6

Tip

Couscous cooks in just 5 minutes, and is an excellent alternative to rice or potatoes. The variations to this dish are endless; add chopped sautéed vegetables, such as carrots and zucchini, for added flavor and a nutritional boost.

Asparagus Vinaigrette with Parmesan and Prosciutto

Makes 4 servings

1 pound asparagus

2 tablespoons fresh lemon juice

1 teaspoon Dijon mustard

¼ teaspoon sugar

¼ teaspoon salt

¼ teaspoon freshly ground pepper

1 tablespoon olive oil

2 paper-thin slices prosciutto or Parma ham (about 1 ounce), finely chopped

1 tablespoon grated Parmesan cheese

1. If the asparagus spears are more than ½″ thick, peel them. In a large skillet of boiling water, cook the asparagus until tender, about 5 minutes. Drain and rinse under cold running water; pat dry and transfer to a wide bowl or platter.

2. Meanwhile, in a small bowl, whisk the lemon juice, mustard, sugar, salt and pepper with 1 tablespoon water; slowly whisk in the oil. Drizzle the dressing over asparagus; sprinkle with the prosciutto and cheese.

Per serving: 78 CALORIES, 5 G TOTAL FAT, 1 G SATURATED FAT, 8 MG CHOLESTEROL, 343 MG SODIUM, 5 G TOTAL CARBOHYDRATE, 2 G DIETARY FIBER, 5 G PROTEIN, 41 MG CALCIUM.

POINTS PER SERVING: 2

Tip

This simple side dish can also double as an elegant appetizer. You can also drizzle the mild lemon-mustard vinaigrette over your favorite combination of greens, or other veggies—try steamed green beans, carrots or beets.

Raspberries with Citrus Sauce

Makes 4 servings

3 tablespoons orange juice
2 tablespoons sugar
2 tablespoons fresh lemon juice
1 tablespoon fresh lime juice
1½ teaspoons cornstarch
½ teaspoon grated orange zest
½ teaspoon grated lemon zest
½ teaspoon grated lime zest
3 cups raspberries

In a small saucepan over medium heat, whisk the orange juice, sugar, lemon juice, lime juice, cornstarch, all three kinds of zest and ⅓ cup cold water, blending until the cornstarch dissolves. Cook, stirring constantly, until thickened, about 3 minutes. Serve the berries, topped with the sauce.

Per serving: 93 Calories, 0 g Total Fat, 0 g Saturated Fat, 0 mg Cholesterol, 0 mg Sodium, 23 g Total Carbohydrate, 5 g Dietary Fiber, 1 g Protein, 38 mg Calcium.

POINTS PER SERVING: 1

Tip

If you like, substitute fresh blackberries for the raspberries. This sauce is also delicious spooned over fat-free pound cake.

A Provençal Feast

A good friend of mine has a villa in the hills of Provence; I have been a visitor there countless times. In Provence, magic comes up with the sun. The setting simply feeds the senses. Green olive trees, blue swimming pools and a virtual symphony of smells: pine, eucalyptus, wild rosemary.

I love the beauty of Provence and the heady scent of the countryside after a rainstorm. I paint a good deal when I am in the French countryside. I try to capture every image in order to create magic in my head, which hopefully flows into my brushes and my life.

Serves 6

Mediterranean Fisherman's Stew

Tarte Provençale

Crusty Baguette*

Assorted Cheese and Fruit Platter*

Mediterranean Fisherman's Stew

Makes 6 servings

One 7-ounce jar roasted red peppers, rinsed and drained

½ cup tomato sauce

2 garlic cloves, peeled

½ teaspoon dried thyme

½ teaspoon dried oregano

2 cups fish broth or clam juice

½ cup dry white wine

1 small onion, chopped

1 bay leaf

12 littleneck clams (about 1 pound), scrubbed

12 mussels (about ¾ pound), scrubbed and debearded

1 pound monkfish, cut into 2" pieces

½ pound medium shrimp, peeled and deveined

12 kalamata olives, halved lengthwise and pitted

2 tablespoons anise-flavored liqueur

¼ teaspoon crushed red pepper flakes, or to taste

1. In a food processor or blender, combine the roasted red peppers, tomato sauce, garlic, thyme and oregano; puree.
2. Transfer the puree to a large nonreactive Dutch oven. Cook, stirring occasionally, until the flavors are blended, about 5 minutes. Stir in the broth, wine, onion, bay leaf and ½ cup water; bring to a boil. Add the clams and mussels; cook, covered, until most of the shells have opened, 6–7 minutes. Remove and discard any clams or mussels whose shells remain closed.
3. Stir in the monkfish, shrimp, olives and liqueur; cook, covered, until the monkfish is opaque and the shrimp pink, 3–4 minutes. Discard the bay leaf; sprinkle with the pepper flakes.

Per serving: 198 Calories, 4 g Total Fat, 0 g Saturated Fat, 95 mg Cholesterol, 450 mg Sodium, 8 g Total Carbohydrate, 2 g Dietary Fiber, 26 g Protein, 85 mg Calcium.

POINTS PER SERVING: 4

—— Tip ——

This unique seafood stew has a less pervasive tomato taste than the more common bouillabaisse; it derives its tangier Mediterranean accent from roasted red pepper and olives. The liqueur is an easy way to get the flavor of fennel without having to crush seeds. Fish broth is available frozen or in bouillon cubes; bottled clam juice may be substituted. For quicker preparation, buy debearded mussels from your fishmonger. Remember to provide bowls for clam and mussel shells.

Tarte Provençale

Makes 6 servings

1 medium (about 1¼-pound) eggplant, cut crosswise into ¼" slices
½ teaspoon salt
¼ teaspoon freshly ground pepper
2 teaspoons olive oil
Two 14½-ounce cans diced tomatoes
1 cup sliced mushrooms
2 tablespoons chopped basil
2 tablespoons capers, rinsed and drained
1 tablespoon chopped oregano
1 tablespoon minced thyme
2 garlic cloves, minced
3 ounces Montrachet (goat cheese), cut into ¼" slices

1. Adjust the oven rack to divide the oven in half. Spray a nonstick baking sheet with nonstick cooking spray; preheat the broiler. Place the eggplant on the baking sheet; sprinkle with ¼ teaspoon of the salt and ⅛ teaspoon of the pepper. Broil until lightly browned, about 2–3 minutes on each side. Remove the eggplant from the broiler. Reduce the oven temperature to 450° F.

2. Meanwhile, in a large nonstick skillet, heat the oil. Cook the tomatoes, mushrooms, basil, capers, oregano, thyme, garlic, the remaining ¼ teaspoon of salt and ⅛ teaspoon of pepper, stirring as needed, until thickened, 5–10 minutes. Remove from the heat.

3. Spray a 9" flameproof pie plate with nonstick cooking spray. Spread the pie plate with one-third of the tomato sauce; top with half of the eggplant slices, overlapping as necessary; repeat the layers, pouring the last third of the tomato sauce over the eggplant. Arrange the goat cheese over the sauce. Bake until the cheese is melted and the edges of the tart are bubbling, about 10

minutes. Increase the oven temperature to broil; broil the tart 4″ from the heat until the cheese is golden brown, 1–2 minutes.

Per serving: 119 CALORIES, 8 G TOTAL FAT, 3 G SATURATED FAT, 11 MG CHOLESTEROL, 527 MG SODIUM, 9 G TOTAL CARBOHYDRATE, 2 G DIETARY FIBER, 5 G PROTEIN, 96 MG CALCIUM.

POINTS PER SERVING: 3

Tip

Try goat cheese flavored with dill or cracked black or red pepper for a subtly different flavor.

A Simple Pasta Dinner

I have had a good deal written about my life in the press. Yet, without doubt, the most hurtful comments have focused on my weight, the hobgoblin I have fought since my teenage years. Although I have tried countless fad diets, I calmed down during my courtship with Andrew, who took me as I was. I recall in an interview before our wedding, I dismissed my battle of the bulge: "I'm not going to get thin. I'm not going to change a lot. I'm just going to be me."

Fact was, as long as my life was in control, so was my weight. When my life was in disarray, my weight followed suit. But who can ever say their life is *always* under control?

I have learned that knowledge is just one way to take control of your life. In those bleak days, I felt a pasta dinner was the enemy that would blow me up for no less than three days. Now, I know that almost any food can be eaten when you are trying to lose weight. You just must remember portion size—and control!

Serves 4

Linguine Riviera

Roasted Pepper Salad

Fresh Fig and Pear Plate*

Linguine Riviera

Makes 4 servings

6 ounces linguine

2 teaspoons olive oil

1 onion, chopped

3 garlic cloves, minced

3 medium zucchini, quartered lengthwise and thinly sliced

2 tomatoes, seeded and diced

1 tablespoon balsamic vinegar

½ teaspoon salt

4 teaspoons grated Parmesan cheese

1. Cook the linguine according to package directions; drain.
2. In a large nonstick saucepan or Dutch oven, heat the oil. Sauté the onion and garlic until softened, about 3 minutes. Stir in the zucchini and sauté until softened, about 3 minutes.
3. Stir in the tomatoes, vinegar and salt; cook, stirring as needed, until the sauce thickens slightly, about 5 minutes. Stir in the linguine; cook, tossing constantly, until heated through, 2–3 minutes. Serve, topped with the cheese.

Per serving: 231 Calories, 4 g Total Fat, 1 g Saturated Fat, 1 mg Cholesterol, 311 mg Sodium, 42 g Total Carbohydrate, 3 g Dietary Fiber, 8 g Protein, 58 mg Calcium.

POINTS PER SERVING: 4

Tip

Fresh basil is a nice addition to this recipe. Add ½ cup of minced fresh leaves or 1–2 tablespoons dried when you stir in the linguine.

Red Potatoes with Caviar and Cheese

Makes 12 servings

12 new red potatoes (about 1 pound), scrubbed
3 tablespoons Neufchâtel cheese
1 tablespoon low-fat (1%) buttermilk
1 teaspoon chopped dill
1 tablespoon black lumpfish caviar

1. Place the potatoes in a single layer in a shallow microwavable container; cook on High until fork-tender, about 3 minutes. Alternately, bake the potatoes at 350° F for 20 minutes.
2. Cut the potatoes in half; place, cut-side down, on a platter. With a spoon or a melon baller, make a small well in the top of each potato.
3. In a small bowl, mix the cheese and buttermilk until smooth; with a rubber spatula, fold in the dill and caviar. Dollop about ¾ teaspoon of the mixture into the well of each potato.

Per serving: 54 CALORIES, 1 G TOTAL FAT, 1 G SATURATED FAT, 11 MG CHOLESTEROL, 39 MG SODIUM, 10 G TOTAL CARBOHYDRATE, 1 G DIETARY FIBER, 2 G PROTEIN, 12 MG CALCIUM.

POINTS PER SERVING: 1

Tip

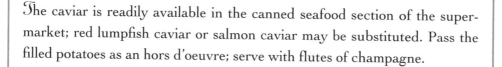

The caviar is readily available in the canned seafood section of the supermarket; red lumpfish caviar or salmon caviar may be substituted. Pass the filled potatoes as an hors d'oeuvre; serve with flutes of champagne.

Tricolor Salad with Gorgonzola Dressing

Makes 12 servings

1 cup crumbled Gorgonzola cheese

¼ cup + 2 tablespoons white-wine vinegar

¼ cup olive oil

3 tablespoons dry white wine

1 tablespoon Dijon mustard

½ teaspoon salt

Freshly ground pepper, to taste

3 heads radicchio, cleaned and torn into bite-size pieces

3 bunches arugula, cleaned and torn into bite-size pieces

1 head Boston or Bibb lettuce, cleaned and torn into bite-size pieces

1. In a blender or food processor, combine the cheese, vinegar, oil, wine, mustard, salt and pepper; pulse until the dressing is creamy and smooth, 4–5 times.
2. In a large salad bowl, combine the radicchio, arugula and lettuce. Drizzle with the dressing; toss to coat.

Per serving: 101 Calories, 8 g Total Fat, 3 g Saturated Fat, 8 mg Cholesterol, 208 mg Sodium, 4 g Total Carbohydrate, 1 g Dietary Fiber, 4 g Protein, 133 mg Calcium.

POINTS PER SERVING: 2

Tip

If this combination of lettuces doesn't strike your fancy, use a mixture of red leaf lettuce, green leaf lettuce and endive, or watercress, romaine and frisée, for alternatives to the three colors.

Lamb Chops with Mint Salsa

Makes 12 servings

12 plum tomatoes, chopped
2 yellow bell peppers, seeded and diced
2 onions, chopped
¼ cup + 2 tablespoons chopped mint
¼ cup fresh lime juice
2 tablespoons olive oil
3–4 garlic cloves, minced
½ teaspoon salt
½ teaspoon freshly ground pepper
¼–½ teaspoon crushed red pepper flakes
Twelve 4-ounce loin lamb chops, ¾" thick

1. In a large nonreactive bowl, mix the tomatoes, bell peppers, onions, mint, lime juice, oil, garlic, salt, pepper and pepper flakes. Let stand at room temperature until the flavors are blended, about 1 hour.
2. Spray a broiler rack with nonstick cooking spray; preheat the broiler. Broil the lamb chops, turning once, 5–6 minutes on each side. Serve with the salsa on the side.

Per serving: 245 CALORIES, 13 G TOTAL FAT, 4 G SATURATED FAT, 81 MG CHOLESTEROL, 211 MG SODIUM, 5 G TOTAL CARBOHYDRATE, 1 G DIETARY FIBER, 26 G PROTEIN, 29 MG CALCIUM.

POINTS PER SERVING: 6

Tip

This unusual salsa combines the coolness of mint with the heat of red pepper. Make it up to two days ahead and store it, covered, in the refrigerator.

Orzo Pilaf

Makes 12 servings

2¼ cups orzo

2 tablespoons olive oil

2 onions, chopped

2 celery stalks, chopped

3–4 garlic cloves, minced

3 cups packed chopped cleaned spinach leaves

¾ cup chicken broth

1½ tablespoons red-wine vinegar

¾ cup grated Asiago cheese

Freshly ground pepper, to taste

1. Cook the orzo according to package directions; drain.
2. Meanwhile, in a large nonstick saucepan or Dutch oven, heat the oil. Sauté the onions, celery and garlic until softened, 5–8 minutes. Stir in the spinach, about ⅓ cup of the broth and the vinegar; cook, stirring frequently, until the liquid evaporates, 3–5 minutes longer. Stir in the orzo, cheese, pepper and the remaining broth.

Per serving: 217 CALORIES, 5 G TOTAL FAT, 1 G SATURATED FAT, 5 MG CHOLESTEROL, 176 MG SODIUM, 35 G TOTAL CARBOHYDRATE, 2 G DIETARY FIBER, 8 G PROTEIN, 99 MG CALCIUM.

POINTS PER SERVING: 4

Tip

If you're in a time crunch, frozen chopped spinach works, too. Just be sure to thaw it completely and squeeze out any excess moisture.

Individual Ginger-Peach Soufflés

Makes 12 servings

12 ounces dried peaches
1 cup + 6 tablespoons sugar
1½ tablespoons all-purpose flour
3 tablespoons brandy
1 tablespoon ground ginger
12 large egg whites, at room temperature
1 tablespoon confectioners' sugar

1. In a medium saucepan, combine the peaches, 1 cup of the sugar and 2¼ cups water, stirring until the sugar dissolves; bring to a boil. Reduce the heat and simmer, covered, until the peaches are very soft, 25–30 minutes.

2. Meanwhile, spray twelve 1-cup soufflé dishes lightly with nonstick cooking spray, spreading with your fingers to coat the dishes evenly; dust each with 1 teaspoon of the remaining sugar. Preheat the oven to 375° F.

3. Transfer the peach mixture to a food processor or blender; puree (you should have 2¼ cups puree; if necessary, add sufficient boiling water to reach that volume).

4. Return the puree to the saucepan; stir in the flour and 2 tablespoons water. Cook over low heat, stirring constantly, until the mixture just begins to give off steam, about 2 minutes. Remove from the heat; stir in the brandy and ginger.

5. In 1 very large bowl or 2 large bowls, beat the egg whites until soft peaks form. Add the remaining 2 tablespoons of sugar and beat until stiff, glossy peaks form.

6. Transfer the peach puree to a very large mixing bowl. Mix in one-third of the egg whites until thoroughly incorporated; with a rubber spatula, gently fold in the remaining egg whites. Divide evenly among the soufflé dishes. With the rubber spatula, make a shallow ridge around the inside rim of each dish. Place the soufflés on a 15 x 20" baking sheet. Bake until the tops are puffed

and browned, 18–20 minutes. Put the confectioners' sugar in a small sieve and dust the soufflés as they come out of the oven. Serve at once.

Per serving: 189 CALORIES, 0 G TOTAL FAT, 0 G SATURATED FAT, 0 MG CHOLESTEROL, 57 MG SODIUM, 42 G TOTAL CARBOHYDRATE, 2 G DIETARY FIBER, 5 G PROTEIN, 11 MG CALCIUM.

POINTS PER SERVING: 3

Tip

For best results, execute Steps 1 through 4 before sitting down to dinner. If desired, the peach puree can be made up to 24 hours in advance and refrigerated. Beating this volume of egg whites will require at least a 5½-quart bowl. If you don't have two bowls that large, beat the egg whites in 2 equal batches; save your biggest bowl for Step 6. Three 1-quart soufflé dishes can be used instead of twelve 1-cup dishes; the baking time remains the same.

A Birthday Gala

Dads was always a major romantic. When I was a small child, he would flood me with birthday cards—not just from him and Mum, but also "signed" by the cat, the dog, the ponies, the house and even the car! Birthdays are still very special days—especially my children's birthdays. I always make an extra effort to be around and celebrate with them. I love to watch their faces light up with glee and excitement, which always gives me such a great sense of pride and pleasure.

Serves 10

Dilly Dip and Vegetables

Honey-Dipped Crunchy Chicken Nuggets

Celebration Birthday Cake

Sugar Cookies

Chocolate-Coconut Fruit Kebabs

Strawberry Lemonade

Dilly Dip and Vegetables

Makes 10 servings

¾ cup light sour cream

1 cucumber, peeled, seeded and finely chopped

2 tablespoons chopped dill

2 tablespoons cider vinegar

1 teaspoon sugar

1 teaspoon Dijon mustard

¼ teaspoon salt

1 head green-leaf lettuce, cleaned and separated

1 small head red cabbage

1 green bell pepper

1 red bell pepper

1 yellow bell pepper

1 orange bell pepper

2 carrots, peeled and cut into sticks

2 celery stalks, cut into sticks

1 cup cauliflower florets

1. In a medium bowl, mix the sour cream, cucumber, dill, vinegar, sugar, mustard and salt. Refrigerate, covered, until ready to use.
2. Line a flat basket or platter with the lettuce leaves. Hollow out the center of the cabbage; place it in the center of the leaves.
3. Holding each pepper upright, cut off the four sides; discard the core with the seeds and membranes. With cookie cutters, cut the peppers into shapes; thread onto bamboo skewers and arrange in the basket with the carrot sticks, celery sticks and cauliflower florets.
4. Just before serving, fill the hollowed-out cabbage with the dip.

Continued on next page.

Per serving: 66 CALORIES, 2 G TOTAL FAT, 0 G SATURATED FAT, 6 MG CHOLESTEROL, 91 MG SODIUM, 11 G TOTAL CARBOHYDRATE, 3 G DIETARY FIBER, 3 G PROTEIN, 71 MG CALCIUM.

POINTS PER SERVING: 1

──────────── Tip ────────────

Get out your favorite animal cookie cutters and let the kids have fun making animal shapes out of veggies. They'll never know this is good-for-you party food.

Honey-Dipped Crunchy Chicken Nuggets

Makes 10 servings

3 tablespoons honey
1 egg white, lightly beaten
2 pounds skinless boneless chicken breasts, cut into 1½″ chunks
1 cup cornflake crumbs
½ teaspoon salt
½ cup reduced-calorie mayonnaise
¼ cup Dijon mustard

1. Preheat the oven to 400° F; spray a large baking sheet with nonstick cooking spray. In a large bowl, mix 1 tablespoon of the honey and the egg white; add the chicken and stir to coat. Transfer the chicken to a colander and set over a large bowl.
2. On a sheet of wax paper, combine the cornflake crumbs and salt. One at a time, dip the chicken pieces into the crumbs, then place on the baking sheet. Spray the tops of the chicken lightly with nonstick cooking spray. Bake until the chicken is cooked through, 8–10 minutes.
3. Meanwhile, in a small bowl, mix the mayonnaise, mustard and the remaining 2 tablespoons of honey. Serve the chicken nuggets with the dipping sauce.

Per serving: 192 CALORIES, 7 G TOTAL FAT, 1 G SATURATED FAT, 55 MG CHOLESTEROL, 332 MG SODIUM, 11 G TOTAL CARBOHYDRATE, 0 G DIETARY FIBER, 21 G PROTEIN, 19 MG CALCIUM.

POINTS PER SERVING: 4

Tip

Freeze the leftovers, if there are any! Thaw them completely, then reheat at 350° F and enjoy.

Celebration Birthday Cake

Makes 12 servings

3 egg whites
2 tablespoons vegetable oil
One 18.25-ounce box reduced-fat devil's food cake mix
1¾ cups reduced-fat ready-to-serve vanilla frosting
1 cup sliced strawberries
Assorted tubes frosting gel
Assorted candy rosettes and cake decorations

1. Preheat the oven to 350° F. Spray two 9" round pans with nonstick cooking spray. Using the egg whites, oil and 1⅓ cups water, prepare the cake mix according to package directions; transfer the batter to the pans. Bake until a tester inserted in the center of the cakes comes out clean, 25–30 minutes. Cool the cakes in the pans 5 minutes, then invert onto wire racks to cool completely.

2. To assemble the cake, place one cake layer, bottom-side up, on a cake stand or large round platter; slide strips of wax paper under the bottom of the cake. Using ½ cup of the frosting, frost the top of the layer; top with the strawberries. Place the remaining cake layer over the berries, bottom-side up. Spread the top and sides of the cake with the remaining frosting; with the frosting gel, write the message, then decorate with the rosettes and cake decorations. Gently remove the wax paper strips from under the cake. Refrigerate until ready to serve.

Per serving: 458 CALORIES, 11 G TOTAL FAT, 3 G SATURATED FAT, 0 MG CHOLESTEROL, 473 MG SODIUM, 86 G TOTAL CARBOHYDRATE, 2 G DIETARY FIBER, 3 G PROTEIN, 78 MG CALCIUM.

POINTS PER SERVING: 10

Tip

Frosting the layers bottom-side up ensures that the top of the cake will be flat and smooth. Buy a 16-ounce can of frosting; use the remaining ¼ cup to frost the cookies.

Sugar Cookies

Makes about 30 cookies

¾ cup all-purpose flour
½ teaspoon baking powder
¼ teaspoon salt
¼ cup + 2 tablespoons sugar
2½ tablespoons butter or margarine
2 tablespoons fat-free egg substitute
½ teaspoon vanilla extract
¼ cup reduced-fat ready-to-serve vanilla frosting
Assorted colored sugars

1. Preheat the oven to 375° F. In a small bowl, combine the flour, baking powder and salt. In a medium bowl, with an electric mixer on medium speed, beat the sugar and butter until light and fluffy. Beat in the egg substitute and vanilla; stir in the flour mixture.

2. On a lightly floured surface, turn out the dough. If necessary, knead in up to 2 tablespoons flour, 1 tablespoon at a time, to make a firm dough. Roll out to ⅛″ thick. Dip 2″ cookie cutters in flour; cut the dough into shapes. Transfer the cookies to a large nonstick baking sheet. Bake until the cookies are lightly golden on the bottom, 8–10 minutes. Cool completely on wire racks.

3. With a small pastry brush, brush the cookies with the frosting; if necessary, thin the frosting with a little water. Sprinkle the cookies with the colored sugars.

Per cookie: 45 CALORIES, 1 G TOTAL FAT, 1 G SATURATED FAT, 3 MG CHOLESTEROL, 49 MG SODIUM, 8 G TOTAL CARBOHYDRATE, 0 G DIETARY FIBER, 0 G PROTEIN, 1 MG CALCIUM.

POINTS PER COOKIE: 1

Tip

Bake and decorate the sugar cookies a day ahead. Place them in a single layer on a wire rack and cover loosely with plastic wrap. Cookies cut in fanciful shapes lend a festive air to a party; if you like, use 2″ alphabet cookie cutters and cut out "Happy Birthday" and your child's name.

Chocolate-Coconut Fruit Kebabs

Makes 10 servings

1 small honeydew melon, seeded and cut into chunks
1 small cantaloupe, seeded and cut into chunks
2 bananas, cut into chunks
3 cups strawberries, hulled (leave whole)
3 tablespoons maple syrup
¼ cup sweetened shredded coconut
Two 1-ounce squares semisweet chocolate, melted

On each of twenty 8″ bamboo skewers, alternately thread the honeydew, cantaloupe, bananas and strawberries. Brush the tops of the kebabs with the syrup; sprinkle with the coconut, then drizzle with the chocolate.

Per serving: 142 CALORIES, 3 G TOTAL FAT, 2 G SATURATED FAT, 0 MG CHOLESTEROL, 37 MG SODIUM, 31 G TOTAL CARBOHYDRATE, 4 G DIETARY FIBER, 2 G PROTEIN, 26 MG CALCIUM.

POINTS PER SERVING: 2

Tip

Here is a dessert that kids will love to put together themselves. After you peel and seed the fruit, let the kids have fun garnishing (and eating!) with the chocolate and coconut. If you don't have 2 squares of chocolate, melt ½ cup chocolate chips instead.

Strawberry Lemonade

Makes 8 servings

3 cups strawberries, halved

1½ cups sugar

1½ cups fresh lemon juice (about 8 lemons)

2 tablespoons grated lemon zest

Mint sprigs, to garnish

In a food processor or blender, puree the strawberries and sugar. Transfer to a large pitcher; blend in 2 cups cold water, the lemon juice and lemon zest. Pour into tall glasses over ice; garnish with the mint sprigs.

Per serving: 174 CALORIES, 0 G TOTAL FAT, 0 G SATURATED FAT, 0 MG CHOLESTEROL, 2 MG SODIUM, 46 G TOTAL CARBOHYDRATE, 2 G DIETARY FIBER, 1 G PROTEIN, 13 MG CALCIUM.

POINTS PER SERVING: 3

Tip

If you're serving more than eight, make this in two batches rather than one double batch unless you have a very large pitcher. For a sophisticated adult drink, stir in 1 cup water and 1 cup vodka instead of the 2 cups water. Using raspberries in lieu of the strawberries would be quite tasty, but you will need to strain the fruit puree through a cheesecloth-lined sieve to eliminate the seeds.

Saturday Night Supper
and Videos

I love watching videos and all kinds of films. Some of my fondest memories of my life at Sunninghill Park involve being with Andrew and the girls, simply watching videos as a family.

Some favorite films that come to mind are *Braveheart* with Mel Gibson and *The Shawshank Redemption* with Morgan Freeman and Tim Robbins. *Dances with Wolves* also holds a special place in my heart. I enjoy films that are purely entertaining and fun: they allow me to escape from the realities of life for a few hours. But I also enjoy movies that revolve around stories of those who have overcome adversity and learned something about themselves or their worlds. Once you discover who you truly are and what your real needs are, then, I believe, you can live a truly happy life.

Serves 4

Tuscan Soup

Mixed Green Salad with Orange Dressing

Balsamic Strawberries

Tuscan Soup

Makes 4 servings

2 cups chicken broth
One 15-ounce can cannellini beans, rinsed and drained
One 14½-can diced tomatoes, drained
1 carrot, peeled and chopped
1 white onion, finely chopped
2 garlic cloves, minced
1 pound kale, cleaned and chopped
½ pound low-fat beef or turkey smoked sausage, chopped (optional)
½ teaspoon salt
Freshly ground pepper, to taste
4 teaspoons grated Parmesan cheese

1. In a large saucepan or Dutch oven, combine the broth, beans, tomatoes, carrot, onion and garlic; bring to a boil. Reduce the heat and simmer, covered, until the carrot is tender, about 15 minutes.
2. Stir in the kale and sausage (if using); cook until the kale is tender, about 10 minutes. Add the salt and pepper to taste. Serve, sprinkled with the cheese.

Per serving (with sausage): 247 CALORIES, 4 G TOTAL FAT, 1 G SATURATED FAT, 31 MG CHOLESTEROL, 1,579 MG SODIUM, 32 G TOTAL CARBOHYDRATE, 11 G DIETARY FIBER, 18 G PROTEIN, 193 MG CALCIUM.

POINTS PER SERVING: 3

Tip

Instead of kale, you can substitute such other greens as escarole, Bibb lettuce, Savoy cabbage or mustard greens. Similarly, great Northern, small white beans or navy beans can be used in lieu of the cannellini. Omitting the sausage will bring the *POINTS* per serving down to 2.

Mixed Green Salad with Orange Dressing

Makes 4 servings

1 tablespoon packed dark brown sugar

1 tablespoon Dijon mustard

3 tablespoons orange juice

1 tablespoon white-wine vinegar

4 cups bitter greens salad mix (escarole, romaine and arugula)

¼ cup walnuts, toasted and chopped (optional)

1. In a small bowl, mix the brown sugar and mustard thoroughly; whisk in the orange juice and vinegar.
2. In a salad bowl, combine the greens and walnuts (if using). Drizzle with the dressing; toss to coat.

Per serving (with walnuts): 79 CALORIES, 5 G TOTAL FAT, 0 G SATURATED FAT,
0 MG CHOLESTEROL, 28 MG SODIUM, 7 G TOTAL CARBOHYDRATE, 1 G DIETARY FIBER,
3 G PROTEIN, 40 MG CALCIUM.

POINTS PER SERVING: 2

Tip

For a milder-tasting salad, substitute spinach for the bitter greens. For a more pungent salad, use coarse-grain mustard and add freshly ground black pepper to taste. Toast the nuts in a small skillet, or see Step 1 in the recipe for Frozen Yogurt Sundaes (page 44). If you decide not to use them, you'll save 1 ***POINT***.

A Simple Pasta Dinner

LINGUINE RIVIERA, FRESH FIG AND PEAR PLATE

A Casual Weeknight Supper

CHICKEN CALVADOS, OVEN-ROASTED ROOT VEGETABLES

A Formal Luncheon

CHOCOLATE PROFITEROLES, KIR ROYALE

Cocktails at Six

PARMESAN CHEESE STRAWS AND PINWHEELS,
SPICED OLIVES WITH LEMON AND FENNEL

Cocktails at Six

DUMPLINGS WITH GINGER DIPPING SAUCE,
NOT-SO-DEVILISH DEVILED EGGS, SAUCISSON EN CROÛTE

Après-Ski Lunch

CINNAMON-NUT BAKED APPLE WITH MAPLE GLAZE,
ESPRESSO WITH KAHLÚA CREAM

A Formal Luncheon

ROAST CHICKEN AND CHUTNEY TEA SANDWICH,
MINTED CARROT SALAD WITH LEMON VINAIGRETTE

A Birthday Gala

CELEBRATION BIRTHDAY CAKE, STRAWBERRY LEMONADE

Balsamic Strawberries

Makes 4 servings

4 teaspoons sugar
1 tablespoon balsamic vinegar
4 cups strawberries, quartered
Freshly ground black pepper, to taste

In a medium bowl, mix the sugar and vinegar, stirring until the sugar dissolves. Add the strawberries and pepper; toss to coat. Let stand 20 minutes, tossing occasionally.

Per serving: 62 Calories, 1 g Total Fat, 0 g Saturated Fat, 0 mg Cholesterol, 2 mg Sodium, 15 g Total Carbohydrate, 4 g Dietary Fiber, 1 g Protein, 21 mg Calcium.

POINTS PER SERVING: 1

Tip

For a more substantial dessert, serve this with Almond Biscotti (page 194) and shaved Parmesan or a bit of Brie cheese.

Après-Ski Lunch

I have been lucky enough to ski since an early age. Two of my favorite resorts are in Switzerland, and I have been going there for so many years now that I feel like a local. I have a good many friends there, and I can relax and feel comfortable. When I have a chance, I especially enjoy skiing with Bruno, an avid skier and one of my dearest friends for years.

A lesson I learned while trying to lose weight is that exercise is crucial, but sticking to it can be a challenge. That's precisely why you must discover what it is you love to do. Skiing is a sport I truly enjoy. I feel strong yet graceful when I ski. I also love the freedom of skiing. When it is just me against the elements (and when I maneuver my way down a particularly difficult slope), I feel absolutely and totally triumphant and exhilarated. The immensity of the mountain also gives me a sense of solitude and security. My troubles—and I—feel incredibly small in such peaceful surroundings.

Serves 4

Mushroom-Caraway Soup

Crunchy Sesame Chicken Salad with Ginger Dressing

Cinnamon-Nut Baked Apples with Maple Glaze

Espresso with Kahlúa Cream

Mushroom-Caraway Soup

Makes 4 servings

1 tablespoon olive oil
One 10-ounce package mushrooms, sliced
3 scallions, sliced
4 cups chicken broth
3 medium red potatoes, scrubbed and cut into 1" chunks
½ cup dry white wine
1 teaspoon dried thyme leaves, crumbled
1 teaspoon caraway seeds, crushed
¼ teaspoon salt
¼ cup half-and-half

1. In a large nonstick saucepan or Dutch oven, heat the oil. Sauté the mush-rooms and scallions until the mushroom liquid evaporates, about 10 minutes.
2. Stir in the broth, potatoes, wine, thyme, caraway seeds and salt; bring to a boil. Reduce the heat and simmer, partially covered, until the potatoes are tender, about 20 minutes. Transfer to a blender and remove the knob in the lid; puree. Return the soup to the saucepan; bring back to a boil. Remove from the heat and stir in the half-and-half.

Per serving: 289 CALORIES, 8 G TOTAL FAT, 2 G SATURATED FAT, 24 MG CHOLESTEROL, 1,147 MG SODIUM, 44 G TOTAL CARBOHYDRATE, 5 G DIETARY FIBER, 8 G PROTEIN, 52 MG CALCIUM.

POINTS PER SERVING: 5

Tip

Just a touch of half-and-half makes a big difference in the richness of this comforting, stick-to-your-ribs soup. Removing the knob from the blender's lid lets the steam escape (if it builds up, the lid may pop off).

Crunchy Sesame Chicken Salad with Ginger Dressing

Makes 4 servings

3 tablespoons sesame seeds

½ teaspoon salt

¼ teaspoon freshly ground pepper

Four 4-ounce skinless boneless chicken breasts

1 tablespoon vegetable oil

2 tablespoons rice-wine vinegar

2 tablespoons reduced-sodium soy sauce

1 tablespoon honey

2 teaspoons grated peeled gingerroot

1 teaspoon mustard powder

1 teaspoon Asian sesame oil

¼ teaspoon crushed red pepper flakes

½ pound baby greens or mesclun

1. In a small bowl, mix the sesame seeds, salt and pepper. Place the chicken on a sheet of wax paper; sprinkle on both sides with the sesame-seed mixture.
2. In a large nonstick skillet, heat the vegetable oil. Sauté the chicken until cooked through, 4–6 minutes on each side. Transfer the chicken to a plate.
3. Meanwhile, in a small saucepan, combine the vinegar, soy sauce, honey, gingerroot, mustard, sesame oil and pepper flakes; bring just to a boil. Remove from the heat.
4. Divide the greens among 4 salad plates. Cut each chicken breast into fourths on the diagonal. Keeping the slices together, arrange the chicken over the greens. Drizzle with the dressing.

Per serving: 251 CALORIES, 11 G TOTAL FAT, 2 G SATURATED FAT, 69 MG CHOLESTEROL, 611 MG SODIUM, 9 G TOTAL CARBOHYDRATE, 2 G DIETARY FIBER, 28 G PROTEIN, 122 MG CALCIUM.

POINTS PER SERVING: 6

Tip

This main-dish salad can be served either warm or cold. Be sure to sprinkle the chicken with the sesame seeds instead of dredging it in them; otherwise, you'll use more sesame seeds than you really need.

Cinnamon-Nut Baked Apples with Maple Glaze

Makes 4 servings

¼ cup packed light brown sugar
1 tablespoon chopped walnuts
½ teaspoon cinnamon
4 large baking apples (we like Rome)
1 tablespoon reduced-calorie margarine
2 tablespoons maple syrup
Cinnamon sticks, to garnish

1. Preheat the oven to 375° F; place ¼ cup water in an 8″ square baking dish.
2. In a small bowl, mix the brown sugar, walnuts and cinnamon. With a small knife, core the apples, but do not cut all the way through the bottoms; peel about ½″ of skin from the top of the apples. Place the apples in the baking dish. Fill each apple with the brown-sugar mixture; dot with the margarine, then drizzle with the maple syrup. Bake, basting the apples occasionally with the pan juices, until just tender, about 40 minutes.
3. With a slotted spoon, transfer the apples to dessert plates. Pour the pan juices over the apples. If you like, garnish each apple with a cinnamon stick.

Per serving: 223 CALORIES, 3 G TOTAL FAT, 0 G SATURATED FAT, 0 MG CHOLESTEROL, 39 MG SODIUM, 52 G TOTAL CARBOHYDRATE, 6 G DIETARY FIBER, 1 G PROTEIN, 41 MG CALCIUM.

POINTS PER SERVING: 4

Tip

Be sure to use baking apples for this, since they'll retain their shape and flavor. Besides Rome, look for Northern Spy, Cortland and Winesap.

Espresso with Kahlúa Cream

Makes 4 servings

½ cup skim milk
1 tablespoon sugar
3 tablespoons Kahlúa or other coffee-flavored liqueur
1½ cups brewed hot espresso
Dash ground nutmeg

1. In a small saucepan over medium heat, combine the milk and sugar, stirring until the sugar dissolves; bring just to a boil. Remove from the heat; add the liqueur, whisking vigorously until the mixture is frothy.
2. Pour the espresso into demitasse cups; spoon the milk mixture over the coffee, then sprinkle with the nutmeg. Serve at once.

Per serving: 65 Calories, 0 g Total Fat, 0 g Saturated Fat, 0 mg Cholesterol, 19 mg Sodium, 9 g Total Carbohydrate, 0 g Dietary Fiber, 1 g Protein, 40 mg Calcium.

POINTS PER SERVING: 1

Tip

Chocolate-flavored liqueur would be an excellent substitute for the Kahlúa. Or try this iced when the warm days of summer arrive: Combine everything in a blender with ice cubes; whirl until frothy.

An American Barbecue

I have been fortunate enough to have traveled around the world, but America has secured a special place in my travel memories. Like the Irish, the American people have always been extremely warm, kind and hospitable. I wholeheartedly embrace this American characteristic.

I admire the gutsy, positive attitude toward life so many Americans seem to possess. And for someone whose every move and action has been scrutinized (and publicized!), that particularly American trait of always seeing people for who they really are—and not being swayed by the judgment of the press and its opinion—is truly refreshing.

Serves 8

Cowboy Beans

Rainbow Cole Slaw

Roasted Corn on the Cob with Cilantro Butter

Barbecue Beef Sandwiches

Zesty Barbecue Sauce

Sandies

Iced Tea*

Cowboy Beans

Makes 8 servings

6 slices turkey bacon, diced
1 large white onion, chopped
Two 15½-ounce cans pinto beans, rinsed and drained
1 cup beer
½ cup Zesty Barbecue Sauce (page 139)
⅛ teaspoon cayenne pepper

1. In a medium nonstick saucepan, combine the bacon and onion. Cook, stirring constantly, until the onion is translucent and the bacon has just begun to brown on the edges, about 15 minutes.
2. Stir in the beans, beer, barbecue sauce and cayenne; bring to a boil. Reduce the heat and simmer, covered, until the flavors are blended, about 15 minutes. Uncover and increase the heat to medium; cook until most of the liquid is absorbed and the sauce thickens, about 5 minutes longer.

Per serving: 132 CALORIES, 2 G TOTAL FAT, 0 G SATURATED FAT, 8 MG CHOLESTEROL, 398 MG SODIUM, 20 G TOTAL CARBOHYDRATE, 4 G DIETARY FIBER, 6 G PROTEIN, 43 MG CALCIUM.

POINTS PER SERVING: 2

Tip

Don't confuse this chuck-wagon-style dish with its sugary Boston cousin; these beans are firmer and spicier. For best results, use a spicy, tangy sauce, such as the Zesty Barbecue Sauce on page 139.

Rainbow Cole Slaw

Makes 8 servings

2 tablespoons Dijon mustard

1 tablespoon fresh lemon juice

⅔ cup reduced-calorie mayonnaise

½ teaspoon sugar

¼ teaspoon salt

1 small head red cabbage, shredded

1 small head green cabbage, shredded

2 carrots, peeled and shredded

1 yellow bell pepper, seeded and thinly sliced

1 small white onion, thinly sliced

1½ teaspoons celery seeds

1. In a small bowl, whisk the mustard and lemon juice; whisk in the mayonnaise, then the sugar and salt.
2. In a large serving bowl, mix the red cabbage, green cabbage, carrots, bell pepper, onion and celery seeds. Drizzle with the dressing; toss to coat.

Per serving: 123 CALORIES, 7 G TOTAL FAT, 1 G SATURATED FAT, 0 MG CHOLESTEROL, 260 MG SODIUM, 13 G TOTAL CARBOHYDRATE, 3 G DIETARY FIBER, 2 G PROTEIN, 78 MG CALCIUM.

POINTS PER SERVING: 2

Tip

This colorful side dish provides a welcome antidote to a spicy barbecue dinner. The recipe lends itself to many variations: Try substituting a head of bok choy or Chinese cabbage for the red or green cabbage, or a green or red bell pepper for the yellow.

Roasted Corn on the Cob with Cilantro Butter

Makes 8 servings

2 tablespoons unsalted butter, softened
1–2 tablespoons finely chopped cilantro
8 ears corn

1. Preheat the grill, or preheat the oven to 400° F. In a small bowl, mix the butter and cilantro.
2. Gently pull back the corn husks, but don't pull them off completely; remove the silk. Smooth the husks back over the corn, then soak in cold water 10 minutes. Place the corn on the grill and cover; grill, with all the grill vents open, 20–30 minutes, or roast directly on the oven rack 20–30 minutes. Serve with the cilantro butter.

Per serving: 109 Calories, 4 g Total Fat, 2 g Saturated Fat, 8 mg Cholesterol, 14 mg Sodium, 19 g Total Carbohydrate, 2 g Dietary Fiber, 3 g Protein, 3 mg Calcium.

POINTS PER SERVING: 2

Tip

Corn can be grilled in advance and used for a variety of dishes, including salsas, salads, soups and chowders. Once you remove the kernels from the cob, they can be frozen.

Sandies

Makes about 40 cookies

⅔ cup all-purpose flour
½ cup wheat-and-barley cereal nuggets
½ teaspoon baking powder
½ cup packed dark brown sugar
¼ cup granulated sugar
¼ cup unsalted margarine or butter, melted
¼ cup fat-free egg substitute
½ teaspoon vanilla extract

1. Preheat the oven to 375° F; lightly spray 2 nonstick baking sheets with non-stick cooking spray.
2. In a food processor, combine the flour, cereal and baking powder; process until the cereal is finely ground, about 1 minute.
3. In a large mixing bowl, beat the brown sugar, granulated sugar and margarine until totally incorporated. Add the egg substitute and vanilla, beating until light and fluffy. With a wooden spoon, stir in the flour mixture. Drop the dough by the ½ tablespoon onto the baking sheets, making about 40 cookies. Bake until the edges begin to brown and cracks begin to appear on the tops of the cookies, 7–8 minutes. Cool completely on wire racks.

Per cookie: 38 CALORIES, 1 G TOTAL FAT, 0 G SATURATED FAT, 0 MG CHOLESTEROL, 9 MG SODIUM, 6 G TOTAL CARBOHYDRATE, 0 G DIETARY FIBER, 0 G PROTEIN, 6 MG CALCIUM.

POINTS PER COOKIE: 1

Tip

When ground, wheat-and-barley cereal nuggets impart the flavor and texture of nuts, with none of the fat. These sturdy cookies travel well and are ideal for barbecues and picnics. Store the sandies in cookie tins or loosely wrapped in aluminum foil for up to 5 days; they also can be frozen for up to 3 months.

An Ideal Breakfast

Since I am always running about, traveling, in business meetings or at charity engagements, I sometimes find it a struggle to ensure I have three proper meals a day. But I know that three meals are crucial to keep up my energy and help me stay trim, so that I am not bingeing the moment things get hectic.

My favorite breakfast in the world is hardly a culinary masterpiece: boiled eggs and butter on my toast "soldiers"—or pieces of toast that have been cut into strips—just as Dads used to make them.

This, however, is hardly the ideal meal on which to base one's day. Since I travel so much, I try to keep my morning meal light and refreshing. I enjoy a wonderful bowl of fresh fruit salad, whole-wheat toast and my customary cup of weak Earl Grey tea.

Serves 2

Summer Fruit Salad

Whole-Wheat Toast with Marmalade*

The Perfect Pot of Tea*

Summer Fruit Salad

Makes 4 servings

2 peaches, pitted and sliced
1 cup strawberries, hulled and halved
1 cup blueberries
1 cup honeydew chunks
1 tablespoon sugar
1½ teaspoons fresh lemon juice
One 8-ounce tub plain nonfat yogurt
1 tablespoon honey
½ teaspoon vanilla extract

1. In a large bowl, combine the fruit. Sprinkle with the sugar and lemon juice; toss to combine. Let stand at room temperature 30 minutes–1 hour, or refrigerate, covered, 1–2 days.
2. In a small bowl, mix the yogurt, honey and vanilla. Just before serving, pour over the fruit; toss to coat.

Per serving: 127 Calories, 0 g Total Fat, 0 g Saturated Fat, 1 mg Cholesterol, 51 mg Sodium, 29 g Total Carbohydrate, 3 g Dietary Fiber, 4 g Protein, 126 mg Calcium.

POINTS PER SERVING: 2

Tip

To make the perfect pot of tea, fill a teakettle with cold water; bring to a rolling boil. Meanwhile, put a little hot tap water in your teapot and swirl it gently to warm the pot. Put the loose tea in the teapot (the rule of thumb is one heaping teaspoon per person, plus one for the pot). Pour the boiling water into the teapot, then cover and let the tea steep for 5 minutes. Serve the tea with milk and lumps of sugar, if you wish.

Cocktails at Six

I enjoy devoting my time to a number of charities—particularly those that benefit the world's less fortunate children. The focus of the countless events and dinners I attend is, rightly so, to raise money for a good cause.

I love meeting new people at these events. I am always so interested in those I'm talking with that I seldom touch any of the food on my plate. I think you can always learn much from listening to and meeting new people, by hearing new views and ideas.

On the few occasions I can gather friends together, I make sure the conversation and good times are the priorities. The food must be delicious and healthy.

Serves 8—10

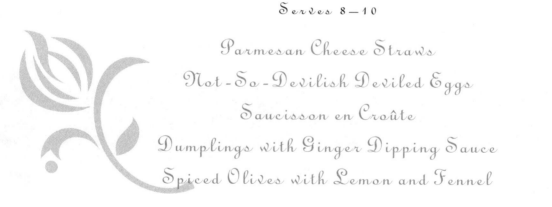

Parmesan Cheese Straws

Not-So-Devilish Deviled Eggs

Saucisson en Croûte

Dumplings with Ginger Dipping Sauce

Spiced Olives with Lemon and Fennel

Parmesan Cheese Straws

Makes 8 servings

½ cup grated Parmesan cheese
2 teaspoons chili powder
½ teaspoon ground cumin
Three 12 x 17″ sheets phyllo dough, at room temperature

1. Preheat the oven to 400° F; spray a large nonstick baking sheet with nonstick cooking spray.
2. In a small bowl, mix the cheese, chili powder and cumin. Place the sheets of phyllo on a work surface and cover them with a damp towel. Remove the first sheet and place it with short side toward you. Coat with nonstick cooking spray (butter-flavored is nice), then sprinkle with about 2 teaspoons of the cheese mixture; fold the phyllo in half to form a 12 x 8½″ rectangle. Spray the phyllo again and sprinkle with 2 more teaspoons of cheese mixture; fold in half again to form a 6 x 8½″ rectangle. Spray again and sprinkle with 2 more teaspoons of cheese mixture; fold in half again to form a 6 x 4¼″ rectangle. Spray again and sprinkle with just a bit of the cheese mixture; with a serrated knife, cut into 8 short strips. Transfer the strips to the baking sheet, placing them about ½″ apart. Repeat the process two more times to make 24 cheese straws. Bake until the cheese straws are crisp and golden, 8–10 minutes. Cool on wire racks.

Per serving: 47 Calories, 2 g Total Fat, 1 g Saturated Fat, 4 mg Cholesterol, 134 mg Sodium, 4 g Total Carbohydrate, 0 g Dietary Fiber, 3 g Protein, 73 mg Calcium.

POINTS PER SERVING: 1

Continued on next page.

Once you've cut the phyllo into straws, form them into different shapes. Twist some as you transfer them to the baking sheet, and roll some into pinwheels. If you're really feeling creative, experiment with bows, hearts or stars. The cheese straws may be stored in an airtight container for 1 week or in the freezer for up to 2 months.

Not-So-Devilish Deviled Eggs

Makes 8 servings

8 hard-cooked eggs, peeled and halved lengthwise
½ cup reduced-calorie mayonnaise
¼ cup low-fat (1%) creamy cottage cheese, drained
1 tablespoon curry powder
1 tablespoon Dijon mustard
Dash hot red pepper sauce
Paprika, for sprinkling
Parsley sprigs, to garnish

1. Place 4 of the eggs yolks in a food processor or blender (discard the other 4) with the mayonnaise, cottage cheese, curry, mustard and pepper sauce; process until blended and smooth.
2. Spoon the filling into a pastry bag with star tip. Pipe the filling into the egg whites, then sprinkle with the paprika. Garnish with the parsley. Refrigerate, covered, until ready to serve.

Per serving: 87 Calories, 6 g Total Fat, 1 g Saturated Fat, 97 mg Cholesterol, 231 mg Sodium, 4 g Total Carbohydrate, 0 g Dietary Fiber, 6 g Protein, 23 mg Calcium.

POINTS PER SERVING: 2

Tip

The food processor gives a very fine, smooth texture to the filling; if you prefer a slightly chunkier texture, use a fork to mash the yolks and mix in the remaining ingredients. Using half the egg yolks and creamy low-fat cottage cheese makes this all-time favorite a fairly virtuous treat. This combination makes a tasty egg salad, too.

Saucisson en Croûte

Makes 8 servings

1 tablespoon oil
One 1-pound bag sauerkraut, rinsed and drained
2 onions, thinly sliced
1 teaspoon caraway seeds
1 pound low-fat turkey kielbasa
One 10-ounce can refrigerated pizza dough
1 cup honey mustard

1. In a large nonstick skillet, heat the oil. Add the sauerkraut, onions, caraway seeds and ½ cup water; cook, covered, until the liquid evaporates and the sauerkraut and onions are very tender, about 15 minutes. Remove from the heat and cool completely.

2. Preheat the oven to 400° F. Cut the kielbasa into two 8″ lengths, then cut the pizza dough in half. On a lightly floured surface, roll out each half of dough into a rectangle about 2″ longer than the kielbasa and wide enough to wrap around it. Spoon half of the sauerkraut mixture down the center of each piece of dough, then place a kielbasa half on the sauerkraut. Fold up the dough to enclose the kielbasa completely, pinching the edges to seal. Transfer to an ungreased baking sheet. Bake until golden, 15–20 minutes. Cut into slices; serve warm or at room temperature, with the honey mustard on the side.

Per serving: 270 CALORIES, 5 G TOTAL FAT, 1 G SATURATED FAT, 26 MG CHOLESTEROL, 975 MG SODIUM, 45 G TOTAL CARBOHYDRATE, 2 G DIETARY FIBER, 14 G PROTEIN, 35 MG CALCIUM.

POINTS PER SERVING: 5

This take on the French classic uses a flavorful low-fat kielbasa, but any already cooked lean sausage would work. Try smoked sausage, or one of those gourmet-style flavored chicken sausages like scallion-and-herb flavor.

Dumplings with Ginger Dipping Sauce

Makes 8 servings

Dipping Sauce

¼ cup red-wine vinegar

¼ cup reduced-sodium soy sauce

2 tablespoons sugar

1 tablespoon Asian sesame oil

1 scallion, thinly sliced

2 teaspoons grated peeled gingerroot

¼ teaspoon crushed red pepper flakes

Dumplings

½ pound lean ground pork

1 scallion, finely minced

1 tablespoon reduced-sodium soy sauce

1 tablespoon Asian sesame oil

1 teaspoon cornstarch

1 teaspoon dry sherry

1 teaspoon grated peeled gingerroot

1 garlic clove, minced

One 12-ounce package (about 48) wonton skins

1. Bring a large pot of water to a boil.
2. In a small bowl, mix the dipping sauce ingredients, stirring until the sugar dissolves; set aside.
3. In a medium bowl, mix the pork, scallion, soy sauce, sesame oil, cornstarch, sherry, gingerroot and garlic.
4. Place the wonton skins on a work surface and cover them with a damp towel. Remove the wonton skins one at a time and place about 1 teaspoon filling in the center; do not overstuff or the wontons won't seal securely. Moisten the

edges of the wontons with water. Bring 2 opposite corners to the center, pinching the points to seal, then bring remaining 2 corners to center, pinching the points to seal. Repeat with the remaining wonton skins and filling.

5. Add the wontons in batches (if you add too many at once they may stick together) to the boiling water. Stir gently with a wooden spoon and bring back to a boil; boil 5 minutes. With a slotted spoon, transfer the wontons to a platter. Serve with dipping sauce.

Per serving: 186 Calories, 6 g Total Fat, 1 g Saturated Fat, 16 mg Cholesterol, 525 mg Sodium, 21 g Total Carbohydrate, 0 g Dietary Fiber, 10 g Protein, 23 mg Calcium.

POINTS PER SERVING: 4

--- *Tip* ---

You'll be surprised how easy these delicate little morsels are to make; if you like, use shrimp or ground skinless turkey or chicken instead of pork. For something different, add the boiled dumplings to your favorite soup. If your supermarket doesn't sell lean ground pork, cut ½ pound pork tenderloin into chunks and grind it in your food processor. Look for wonton skins in the produce department of your supermarket.

Spiced Olives with Lemon and Fennel

Makes 10 servings

1 cup kalamata olives

1 cup oil-cured black olives

1 cup Sicilian (green) olives

1 cup fennel, trimmed and thinly sliced

1 garlic clove, thinly sliced

1 tablespoon grated lemon zest

1 tablespoon chopped fresh rosemary, or 1 teaspoon dried, crumbled

1 tablespoon chopped fresh thyme, or 1 teaspoon dried, crumbled

1 tablespoon fresh lemon juice

1 teaspoon olive oil

In a large bowl, mix all the ingredients. Serve at room temperature.

Per serving: 88 CALORIES, 9 G TOTAL FAT, 1 G SATURATED FAT, 0 MG CHOLESTEROL, 925 MG SODIUM, 3 G TOTAL CARBOHYDRATE, 1 G DIETARY FIBER, 1 G PROTEIN, 43 MG CALCIUM.

POINTS PER SERVING: 2

Tip

Use whatever olives you prefer, as any variety will work well with the other flavors. We don't call for pitted olives, as they wouldn't look as attractive as those left whole. If you've never encountered a fennel bulb before, see Step 2 of the Fennel and Blood Orange Salad recipe (page 63) for trimming how-tos.

A Formal Luncheon

Royal Ascot is the British equivalent of America's Kentucky Derby: a grand social occasion at which parties are held after the races.

In my Mum's day, Ascot was as it is today, a highly fashionable event where the hats receive more notice than the horses. Nowadays, I rarely attend, but I will never forget the first time I went: I spent the week playing games and attending the races, cocktail parties and grand dinners. At times, I felt awkward. Yet that first Ascot was the most memorable and special because out of such humble beginnings came a great and lasting friendship, one that endures to this very day. I came to know Andrew that week.

While the meals I ate that Ascot week were extraordinary, the one thing I remember was the chocolate profiteroles. Andrew and I joked about them over lunch.

Serves 4

Sesame Breadsticks*

Roast Chicken and Chutney Tea Sandwiches

Minted Carrot Salad with Lemon Vinaigrette

Orange Tea Biscuits with Citrus Glaze

Chocolate Profiteroles

Kir Royales

Roast Chicken and Chutney Tea Sandwiches

Makes 4 servings

2 teaspoons vegetable oil
2 onions, chopped
1 teaspoon ground ginger
2 Granny Smith apples, peeled, cored and diced
⅔ cup dried cranberries or raisins
½ cup apple cider
¼ cup cider vinegar
3 tablespoons packed dark brown sugar
8 slices pumpernickel or raisin-pumpernickel bread
½ cup watercress, cleaned and torn
2 cups sliced skinless roast chicken breast

1. In a large nonstick skillet, heat the oil. Add the onions and ginger; cook, stirring as needed, until the onions are tender and lightly browned, about 10 minutes. Add the apples, cranberries, cider, vinegar and brown sugar; reduce the heat and simmer, uncovered, stirring as needed, until the liquid evaporates and the chutney thickens, about 30 minutes. Cool to room temperature, then refrigerate until ready to use.
2. To assemble the sandwiches, line 4 slices of bread with the watercress, then the chicken. Dollop each with 1 tablespoon of the chutney before covering with another slice of bread; cut the sandwiches in half and serve at once.

Per serving: 492 CALORIES, 8 G TOTAL FAT, 2 G SATURATED FAT, 60 MG CHOLESTEROL, 496 MG SODIUM, 80 G TOTAL CARBOHYDRATE, 7 G DIETARY FIBER, 29 G PROTEIN, 99 MG CALCIUM.

POINTS PER SERVING: 9

This easy apple chutney is a great accompaniment for roast pork as well as poultry. Adjust the texture to suit your taste: for a chunky relish, cut the fruit more coarsely, for a jamlike chutney, cut it finer. Make the chutney a day ahead to allow its flavors to develop fully. Refrigerate any leftover chutney in a tightly sealed jar for up to 1 week.

Minted Carrot Salad with Lemon Vinaigrette

Makes 4 servings

2 tablespoons fresh lemon juice
2 teaspoons olive oil
1 teaspoon sugar
4 carrots, shredded
1 cup golden raisins
3 tablespoons chopped mint

1. In a small bowl, mix the lemon juice, oil and sugar.
2. In a large bowl, mix the carrots, raisins and mint. Drizzle with the dressing; toss to coat.

Per serving: 182 Calories, 3 g Total Fat, 0 g Saturated Fat, 0 mg Cholesterol, 32 mg Sodium, 42 g Total Carbohydrate, 4 g Dietary Fiber, 2 g Protein, 46 mg Calcium.

POINTS PER SERVING: 3

Tip

With its hint of mint, this salad is wonderfully refreshing on a hot summer's day. You can serve it right away if you like, but the sweetness of the raisins is more pronounced if you let it stand at room temperature for 30 minutes.

Orange Tea Biscuits with Citrus Glaze

Makes 12 servings

2 cups all-purpose flour
¼ cup granulated sugar
2 teaspoons baking powder
½ teaspoon salt
5 tablespoons cold margarine or butter
½ cup dried currants
½ cup low-fat (1%) buttermilk
2 tablespoons orange juice
1 tablespoon fresh lemon juice
3 tablespoons confectioners' sugar

1. Preheat the oven to 400° F; spray a 12-cup muffin tin with nonstick cooking spray.
2. In a large bowl, mix the flour, granulated sugar, baking powder and salt. With a pastry blender or two knives, cut in the margarine until the mixture resembles coarse crumbs. Stir in the currants and buttermilk until just blended; do not overmix. Spoon the batter into the muffin cups. Bake until golden, 12–15 minutes. Cool on a wire rack 10 minutes.
3. Meanwhile, prepare the glaze. In a small bowl, mix the orange juice and lemon juice; stir in the confectioners' sugar. Brush the tops of the slightly cooled biscuits with the glaze; cool completely before serving.

Per serving: 158 CALORIES, 5 G TOTAL FAT, 1 G SATURATED FAT, 0 MG CHOLESTEROL, 222 MG SODIUM, 26 G TOTAL CARBOHYDRATE, 1 G DIETARY FIBER, 3 G PROTEIN, 50 MG CALCIUM.

POINTS PER SERVING: 3

Continued on next page.

Serve these biscuits with orange marmalade or apricot jam and a pot of Earl Grey or English Breakfast tea. Leftover biscuits may be kept for a few days in an airtight plastic bag.

Chocolate Profiteroles

Makes 8 servings

¼ cup + 4 teaspoons margarine
¾ cup all-purpose flour
2 eggs
¼ cup fat-free egg substitute
⅓ cup sugar
2 tablespoons unsweetened cocoa powder
2 tablespoons cornstarch
1 cup skim milk
2 teaspoons vanilla extract
2 teaspoons confectioners' sugar

1. Preheat the oven to 400° F; spray a large baking sheet with nonstick cooking spray.

2. In a medium saucepan, bring ¾ cup water and ¼ cup of the margarine to a full boil. Stir in the flour; cook, stirring constantly, until the dough pulls away from the sides of the pan, 1–2 minutes. Remove from the heat; stir in the eggs, one at a time, until the dough is smooth. Drop the dough, 1 heaping table-spoon at a time, onto the baking sheet, making 24 balls. (If you prefer, trans-fer the dough to a pastry bag; pipe the dough onto the baking sheet in 1½″ balls.) Bake until golden, 25–30 minutes. Slice a small portion off the top of each puff; cool on a wire rack.

3. Place the egg substitute in a small bowl. In a medium nonstick saucepan, com-bine the sugar, cocoa powder and cornstarch. Stir in the milk, vanilla and ½ cup water; bring to a boil, stirring constantly, and boil 1 minute. Slowly whisk a small amount of the cocoa mixture into the egg substitute, then slowly pour the egg mixture into the cocoa mixture, whisking quickly and constantly. Cook, stirring constantly, until just boiling. Remove from the heat; whisk in

Continued on next page.

the remaining 4 teaspoons of margarine. Transfer the chocolate pastry cream to a bowl; refrigerate, covered, until chilled and thickened, about 2 hours.

4. Spoon the pastry cream into the puffs; replace the tops. Put the confectioners' sugar in a small sieve and shake over the profiteroles. Serve at once.

Per serving: 193 Calories, 7 g Total Fat, 2 g Saturated Fat, 54 mg Cholesterol, 123 mg Sodium, 22 g Total Carbohydrate, 1 g Dietary Fiber, 5 g Protein, 50 mg Calcium.

POINTS PER SERVING: 4

Tip

Profiteroles are miniature cream puffs. Be sure to cut off the tops of the puffs when you remove them from the oven so that steam can escape. If you'd rather not make the pastry cream, fill the profiteroles with nonfat frozen yogurt. They're also delicious drizzled with chocolate syrup.

Kir Royales

Makes 4 servings

8 fresh raspberries
2 teaspoons crème de cassis (black-currant-flavored liqueur)
One 750-milliliter bottle dry champagne, well chilled

Place 2 raspberries in each of 4 champagne flutes; add ½ teaspoon crème de cassis to each. Pour the champagne over and serve at once.

Per serving: 142 CALORIES, 0 G TOTAL FAT, 0 G SATURATED FAT, 0 MG CHOLESTEROL, 0 MG SODIUM, 6 G TOTAL CARBOHYDRATE, 1 G DIETARY FIBER, 0 G PROTEIN, 2 MG CALCIUM.

POINTS PER SERVING: 3

Tip

If you prefer, use sparkling nonalcoholic cider, unflavored seltzer or ginger ale instead of the champagne.

An Argentinean Feast

In the past chapters of my life, my antidote for being unhappy had been food and more food. I remember the menu selections at home suffering after Mum left when I was twelve. I would have sausages for breakfast, then again for a snack, after lunch and at tea, when I would "balance" the meal out with boiled eggs and buttered white toast.

I loved visiting Mum and her new husband, Hector, in Argentina. I remember flying to Buenos Aires, then driving 300 miles across the Pampas, the great plains of South America, to Hector's farm. The country is breathtaking: the air pure and the sky unbroken. We had wonderful times: I rode the polo ponies (Hector was a world-class polo player) and spent a good deal of time with Mum—these are the memories that I cherish most.

Serves 4

Turkey Empanadas

Roasted Pork Loin

Baby Lamb Chops

Classic Roast Beef (served without the Wild Mushrooms) (see page 64)

Quinoa Salad

Shoestring Beets and Arugula Salad

Tarragon Vinaigrette

Alfajores

Turkey Empanadas

Makes 4 servings

1 onion, chopped
2 teaspoons canola oil
½ teaspoon ground allspice
1 garlic clove, minced
1 pound ground skinless turkey breast
1 teaspoon dried oregano
1 teaspoon salt
Twelve 12 x 17″ sheets phyllo dough, at room temperature
¼ cup fat-free egg substitute

1. Preheat a medium skillet over medium heat. Combine the onion, oil, allspice and garlic in the hot skillet; cook, stirring occasionally, until the onion just begins to brown, about 7 minutes. Add the turkey, oregano and salt; cook, breaking apart the turkey with a wooden spoon, until browned, 5–8 minutes. Refrigerate, covered, until the mixture is firm, at least 1 hour.

2. Preheat the oven to 375° F; line a baking sheet with parchment, or line it with foil or wax paper and spray with nonstick spray.

3. Place the sheets of phyllo on a work surface and cover them with a damp towel. Remove the first sheet and spray with nonstick cooking spray (garlic-flavored is nice). Remove a second sheet, lay it directly on top and spray it. Top with a third sheet and spray again. Cut the rectangle into three 5½ x 12″ strips. Put ¼ cup of the turkey filling in the bottom right-hand corner of each strip and fold the dough over the filling to make a triangle. Continue to fold each up like a flag. Repeat the process three more times to make 12 empanadas. Transfer the empanadas to the baking sheet and brush with the egg substitute. Bake until golden brown, 20–25 minutes.

Continued on next page.

Per serving: 333 CALORIES, 6 G TOTAL FAT, 0 G SATURATED FAT, 70 MG CHOLESTEROL, 890 MG SODIUM, 33 G TOTAL CARBOHYDRATE, 1 G DIETARY FIBER, 26 G PROTEIN, 45 MG CALCIUM.

POINTS PER SERVING: 7

--- *Tip* ---

In South America, the customary serving is three empanadas per person; they can also be passed on a platter. The filling can be prepared a day in advance and stored in the refrigerator. Tote any leftovers to the office for a great next-day lunch.

Roasted Pork Loin

Makes 4 servings

One 1–1¼-pound pork tenderloin
1 tablespoon fresh lemon juice
2½ teaspoons olive oil
1 garlic clove, minced
½ teaspoon freshly ground pepper
½ teaspoon ground cumin
½ teaspoon salt
¼ teaspoon cinnamon
¼ teaspoon ground cloves
2 large sweet potatoes, peeled and cut into chunks
1 green bell pepper, seeded, quartered lengthwise, then halved crosswise
One 6-ounce package large pearl onions, peeled

1. Place the pork on a sheet of plastic wrap. In a small bowl, mix the lemon juice, 1 teaspoon of the olive oil, the garlic, pepper, cumin, salt, cinnamon and cloves to make a paste. Rub the paste all over the pork, then wrap in the plastic and refrigerate 1 hour.
2. Preheat the oven to 350° F. Place the tenderloin in a shallow roasting pan. In a large bowl, toss the sweet potatoes, bell pepper and onions in the remaining 1½ teaspoons of oil; scatter around the pork. Roast until the pork reaches an internal temperature of 165° F, about 45 minutes. Transfer to a cutting board and let stand 10 minutes before slicing the pork into ½″ medallions. Serve the vegetables on the side.

Per serving: 355 Calories, 13 g Total Fat, 4 g Saturated Fat, 73 mg Cholesterol, 357 mg Sodium, 26 g Total Carbohydrate, 4 g Dietary Fiber, 32 g Protein, 64 mg Calcium.

POINTS PER SERVING: 7

Continued on next page.

An Argentinean Feast

This is an elegant one-dish meal. The spicy coating on the tenderloin pairs wonderfully with the sweet potatoes. The recipe can easily be doubled, with a second tenderloin, to serve 8.

Baby Lamb Chops

Makes 4 servings

2 garlic cloves, peeled
½ teaspoon kosher salt
Four 4-ounce boneless lamb chops

1. Spray the broiler rack with nonstick cooking spray; preheat the broiler.
2. Place the garlic and salt on a cutting board; with the flat side of a knife, crush to a paste.
3. Broil the lamb 4″ from heat until well browned, 3–4 minutes. Turn the chops over and spread with the paste. Broil until the lamb is cooked through and the paste is browned, 4 minutes longer. Let stand 5 minutes before serving.

Per serving: 202 CALORIES, 11 G TOTAL FAT, 4 G SATURATED FAT, 77 MG CHOLESTEROL, 339 MG SODIUM, 0 G TOTAL CARBOHYDRATE, 0 G DIETARY FIBER, 24 G PROTEIN, 18 MG CALCIUM.

POINTS PER SERVING: 5

Tip

A cleaver or chef's knife is best for crushing the garlic. If you don't have either, use a utensil like a cake server or even the bottom of a metal or plastic measuring cup.

Quinoa Salad

Makes 4 servings

1 cup quinoa, thoroughly rinsed and drained
½ pound fresh peas, shelled
1 roasted red pepper, broken up (about ½ cup)
2 tablespoons fresh lime juice
1 teaspoon dried thyme leaves, crumbled
1 garlic clove, coarsely chopped
¼ teaspoon ground white pepper
¼ teaspoon salt
1 carrot, diced
2 scallions, thinly sliced

1. In a medium saucepan, bring 2 cups water to a boil. Stir in the quinoa and bring back to a boil. Reduce the heat and simmer, covered, until the water is almost absorbed, about 11 minutes. Stir in the peas, re-cover and cook until the peas are bright green, the quinoa looks transparent and the water is completely absorbed, about 2 minutes longer. Transfer to a bowl.

2. To make the dressing, in a food processor, combine the roasted red pepper, lime juice, thyme, garlic, white pepper and salt; puree.

3. Add the carrot, scallions and dressing to the quinoa; toss to combine. Refrigerate, covered, until the flavors are blended, at least 30 minutes.

Per serving: 231 CALORIES, 3 G TOTAL FAT, 0 G SATURATED FAT, 0 MG CHOLESTEROL, 154 MG SODIUM, 44 G TOTAL CARBOHYDRATE, 7 G DIETARY FIBER, 10 G PROTEIN, 60 MG CALCIUM.

POINTS PER SERVING: 3

Quinoa, which was cultivated by the ancient Incas, contains more protein than any other grain. Be sure to rinse the quinoa thoroughly—it has a coating that, if not rinsed off, can make the grain bitter. The fresh peas can be replaced with ½ cup frozen baby peas, completely thawed; add them with the carrot and scallions. The salad can be made in advance and keeps well in the refrigerator for up to 3 days.

Shoestring Beets and Arugula Salad

Makes 4 servings

1 bunch watercress, cleaned and torn
1 bunch arugula, cleaned and torn
1 head Belgian endive, cleaned and cut lengthwise into thin strips
2 cups fresh cooked or drained canned beets, cut into thin strips
1 batch Tarragon Vinaigrette (recipe follows)

On a platter, combine the watercress, arugula and endive; mound the beets in the center, then drizzle with the vinaigrette.

Per serving: 87 Calories, 4 g Total Fat, 0 g Saturated Fat, 0 mg Cholesterol, 240 mg Sodium, 12 g Total Carbohydrate, 3 g Dietary Fiber, 3 g Protein, 113 mg Calcium.

POINTS PER SERVING: 1

_____ Tip _____

If you use fresh beets, cook them according to Step 1 of the recipe for Beet and Apple "Napoleon" (page 201).

Tarragon Vinaigrette

Makes 4 servings

2 tablespoons cider vinegar
1 tablespoon olive oil
2 teaspoons Dijon mustard
¼ teaspoon salt
¼ teaspoon freshly ground pepper
1 tablespoon chopped tarragon

In a small bowl, mix the vinegar, oil, mustard, salt and pepper. Refrigerate, covered, until ready to use. Whisk in the tarragon just before drizzling over the salad.

Per serving: 34 Calories, 4 g Total Fat, 0 g Saturated Fat, 0 mg Cholesterol, 148 mg Sodium, 1 g Total Carbohydrate, 0 g Dietary Fiber, 0 g Protein, 5 mg Calcium.

POINTS PER SERVING: 1

Tip

There is something very special about the combination of fresh tarragon and beets. If you can't find fresh tarragon, substitute 1 teaspoon dried.

Alfajores

Makes 12 servings

One 14-ounce can sweetened condensed skimmed milk
One 3" cinnamon stick
One 8" round sponge cake
¼ teaspoon confectioners' sugar
¼ teaspoon ground cinnamon

1. In a small, heavy saucepan over medium heat, cook the condensed milk, stirring constantly, until liquefied, about 30 seconds. Reduce the heat to the lowest possible setting and add the cinnamon stick; cook, stirring occasionally, until the consistency is custardlike, 2¼–2½ hours. Remove from the heat, discard the cinnamon stick and stir for 1 minute to cool. Transfer the custard to a bowl.

2. Cut the cake twice horizontally to form 3 layers. Spread about ½ cup of the custard between each layer. In a small bowl, mix the confectioners' sugar and cinnamon; dust the top of the cake with the mixture.

Per serving: 154 Calories, 1 g Total Fat, 0 g Saturated Fat, 26 mg Cholesterol, 104 mg Sodium, 34 g Total Carbohydrate, 0 g Dietary Fiber, 4 g Protein, 112 mg Calcium.

POINTS PER SERVING: 3

Tip

Alfajores are usually made as individual pastries. A storebought cake or a cake mix (freezing the second layer) simplifies preparation. Using sweetened condensed milk cuts the cooking time of the custard in half—and the custard, by the way, is delicious on its own.

A Perfect Picnic

I am, without question, an outdoors person. I hate being trapped indoors, and when I am, I soon find myself longing for the quiet fields of Dummer, the soothing rivers of Scotland or the solitude of the mountains.

I will never forget when Andrew and I headed to Canada for our first overseas tour together. We had an exhausting schedule, and after a week, I must say, I wanted nothing more than to head for the nearest beach and collapse. Yet Andrew had a different type of holiday in mind: a two-week canoe trip with a team of six others in the remote Northwest Territories.

When I look back at my diaries from that trip, I am amazed I survived. Never mind the grueling trip down the Hanbury River. There were mosquitoes and blackflies everywhere! For twelve days, we had the same lunch of salami and cheese. And the river was unyielding—enormous and unforgiving.

Nowadays, I try to make sure my picnics are slightly more relaxing!

Serves 4

Chilled Honeydew Soup

Spinach Chicken Salad

Tomato Parmesan Toasts

Mixed Berry Turnovers

Chilled Honeydew Soup

Makes 4 servings

1 small (about 1½-pound) honeydew melon
¾ cup plain nonfat yogurt
1½ tablespoons white-wine vinegar
4 slices hard salami, chopped

1. Peel, seed and cube the melon; you will need 2 cups cubed melon.
2. In a food processor or blender, puree the melon, yogurt and vinegar. Refrigerate, covered, until thoroughly chilled, about 1 hour.
3. Serve the soup in small, chilled bowls. Garnish each serving with about 1 tablespoon of the chopped salami.

Per serving: 83 CALORIES, 3 G TOTAL FAT, 1 G SATURATED FAT, 6 MG CHOLESTEROL, 201 MG SODIUM, 12 G TOTAL CARBOHYDRATE, 1 G DIETARY FIBER, 4 G PROTEIN, 91 MG CALCIUM.

POINTS PER SERVING: 2

Tip

This complex-tasting soup takes only minutes of hands-on preparation. You may have some melon left over; save it for a fruit salad or a snack. If you like, garnish each serving with a dollop of yogurt or ⅓ cup chopped, peeled cucumber in addition to the salami.

Spinach Chicken Salad

Makes 4 servings

¼ cup + 2 tablespoons red-wine vinegar

¼ cup honey

2 tablespoons fresh lemon juice

1 tablespoon packed dark brown sugar

1 tablespoon Dijon mustard

1½ teaspoons Worcestershire sauce

One 10-ounce package triple-washed spinach, stemmed,
leaves broken in half and rinsed

2 cups shredded cooked chicken breast

1 small red onion, thinly sliced

6 slices turkey bacon, cooked crisp

1. In a small saucepan over medium heat, mix the vinegar, honey, lemon juice, brown sugar, mustard and Worcestershire sauce; cook, whisking constantly, until steaming, about 3 minutes.

2. Divide the spinach among 4 salad plates; top with the chicken and onion. Drizzle with the warm dressing, then crumble the bacon over the salads.

Per serving: 326 CALORIES, 5 G TOTAL FAT, 1 G SATURATED FAT, 40 MG CHOLESTEROL, 580 MG SODIUM, 27 G TOTAL CARBOHYDRATE, 2 G DIETARY FIBER, 17 G PROTEIN, 90 MG CALCIUM.

POINTS PER SERVING: 7

Tip

For a novel alternative to chicken, try the salted codfish known as baccalà: Soak ½ pound salt cod overnight in water; drain. Bring 2 cups water to a boil in a medium saucepan, then simmer the cod with 2 celery stalks until the fish is tender and flakes easily, about 10 minutes. Cool the cod, discard the celery, then flake the fish over the spinach.

Tomato Parmesan Toasts

Makes 4 servings

Four ½" slices French baguette
1 teaspoon reduced-calorie margarine
1 Roma or plum tomato, cored and cut lengthwise into 4 slices
1 garlic clove, minced
1 teaspoon grated Parmesan cheese

Preheat the broiler. Lightly toast the baguette slices on one side under the broiler. Flip and coat the untoasted sides with the margarine. Place a slice of tomato on each, then sprinkle with the garlic and cheese. Broil until the bread is toasted on the second side and the cheese is beginning to melt but is not yet browned, about 30 seconds.

Per serving: 46 Calories, 1 g Total Fat, 0 g Saturated Fat, 0 mg Cholesterol, 96 mg Sodium, 8 g Total Carbohydrate, 0 g Dietary Fiber, 2 g Protein, 18 mg Calcium.

POINTS PER SERVING: 1

Tip

We call for Roma, or Italian plum, tomatoes because they have few seeds; beefsteak tomatoes sliced crosswise can be substituted in a pinch. This dish lends itself to a number of variations: Try shredded mozzarella in lieu of the Parmesan, or add a little chopped fresh oregano on top of the cheese. Double or triple the recipe for hors d'oeuvres.

Mixed Berry Turnovers

Makes 4 servings

½ pint blueberries, picked over

½ pint raspberries, picked over

¼ cup + 1 teaspoon sugar

3 tablespoons all-purpose flour

3 tablespoons amaretto liqueur

One 9″ square frozen puff pastry, thawed

2 tablespoons fat-free egg substitute

1. In a small, heavy saucepan over high heat, combine the blueberries, raspberries, and ¼ cup of the sugar; bring to a boil, stirring constantly. Reduce the heat to medium and cook, stirring occasionally, until the berries start to give off juices, about 3 minutes. Meanwhile, in a small bowl, whisk the flour and amaretto to a smooth paste.

2. Remove the berries from the heat and stir in the paste. Return to medium heat and cook, stirring constantly, until thick, about 2 minutes. Transfer to a bowl and place in the freezer until chilled, about 20 minutes.

3. Preheat the oven to 375° F; line a baking sheet with parchment paper, or line it with foil or wax paper and spray with nonstick cooking spray.

4. On a lightly floured surface, roll out the puff pastry to an 11″ square. Cut into four 5½″ squares and brush off any excess flour. Put about ¼ cup of the chilled filling in the center of each square, then brush the outside borders with some of the egg substitute. Fold in half on the diagonal to form a triangle, pressing the edges together.

5. Transfer the turnovers to the baking sheet. Make 3 slits in the top of each turnover with the tip of a sharp knife. Brush the tops of the turnovers with the remaining egg substitute and sprinkle each with ¼ teaspoon of the remaining sugar. Bake until puffed and browned, about 30 minutes. Cool on wire racks.

Continued on next page.

Per serving: 203 Calories, 4 g Total Fat, 1 g Saturated Fat, 0 mg Cholesterol, 41 mg Sodium, 35 g Total Carbohydrate, 3 g Dietary Fiber, 3 g Protein, 13 mg Calcium.

POINTS PER SERVING: 4

—— *Tip* ——

When fresh blueberries and raspberries are out of season, use 1 cup each of frozen berries, thawed and drained. Make sure the slits in the tops of the turnovers are sufficiently small to let out the steam but not the filling.

A Winter Weekend Supper

Drowning my sorrows in food is one habit I have worked diligently at breaking. I remember when I was pregnant and Andrew was away at sea, I numbed my emotions in mayonnaise, sausage rolls and smoked mackerel pâté sandwiches. I got bigger and bigger. Just prior to the birth, I weighed a bit over 200 pounds.

Eating becomes a form of therapy. It is what I call the missing link, the connection between happiness or unhappiness and one's eating habits. When I was tense or aggravated, I used to reach for food instead of trying to uncover the underlying cause of why I was feeling disheartened.

It is critical to resolve those emotional problems that swirl about in your head, nagging and chipping away at your self-esteem and sense of self-worth. Nowadays, I still have my favorite treats, but only because I am physically hungry for food.

Serves 4

Rosemary Roast Chicken

Herbed Parmesan Biscuits

Radicchio Salad

Crumbled Parmesan Vinaigrette

Strawberry - Rhubarb Compote

Rosemary Roast Chicken

Makes 6 servings

2 garlic cloves, peeled
1 tablespoon fresh rosemary, or 1 teaspoon dried
2 teaspoons olive oil
½ teaspoon salt
¼ teaspoon freshly ground pepper
One 3–3½-pound chicken
1 lemon, halved

1. Preheat the oven to 350° F. In a mini food processor, combine the garlic, rosemary, oil, salt and pepper; puree.

2. Rinse the chicken thoroughly inside and out; pat dry with paper towels. Discard the giblets and remove any visible fat. Gently loosen the skin over the breast; rub the rosemary mixture under the skin. Squeeze the lemon over the chicken and place the halves in the cavity. Tuck the wings under the back. Place on a rack in a roasting pan. Roast, basting occasionally with the pan juices, until the juices run clear when the thigh is pierced with a fork, about 1 hour–1 hour 20 minutes. Transfer to a cutting board and let stand 10 minutes before carving. Remove the skin before eating.

Per serving: 201 CALORIES, 8 G TOTAL FAT, 2 G SATURATED FAT, 90 MG CHOLESTEROL, 263 MG SODIUM, 1 G TOTAL CARBOHYDRATE, 0 G DIETARY FIBER, 30 G PROTEIN, 20 MG CALCIUM.

POINTS PER SERVING: 5

Tip

Use any leftover chicken in Roast Chicken Salad (page 200) and Roast Chicken and Chutney Tea Sandwiches (page 154).

Herbed Parmesan Biscuits

Makes 8 servings

1½ cups all-purpose flour
¼ cup + 2 tablespoons grated Parmesan cheese
1 teaspoon baking powder
½ teaspoon baking soda
½ teaspoon dried oregano leaves, crumbled
½ teaspoon fennel seeds
¼ teaspoon salt
¼ teaspoon freshly ground pepper
Pinch cayenne pepper
1 cup plain nonfat yogurt

1. Preheat oven to 425° F; spray a baking sheet with nonstick cooking spray. In a medium bowl, mix the flour, cheese, baking powder, baking soda, oregano, fennel seeds, salt, pepper and cayenne; stir in the yogurt and 2 tablespoons water.
2. On a lightly floured surface, turn out the dough. With lightly floured hands, pat it into a rectangle about ½″ thick; cut into 8 pieces. Transfer to the baking sheet. Bake until the biscuits are golden brown and crispy, about 20 minutes.

Per serving: 140 Calories, 3 g Total Fat, 2 g Saturated Fat, 7 mg Cholesterol, 378 mg Sodium, 21 g Total Carbohydrate, 1 g Dietary Fiber, 8 g Protein, 207 mg Calcium.

POINTS PER SERVING: 3

Tip

No yogurt on hand? Put 1 tablespoon lemon juice or white vinegar in a 1-cup glass measure, then add milk to make 1 cup; let stand 5 minutes before using. Leftover biscuits can be kept in an airtight plastic bag or container for 1 or 2 days. They make a delightful accompaniment to a soup such as Twenty-Minute Minestrone (page 92).

Radicchio Salad

Makes 4 servings

1 head radicchio
1 batch Crumbled Parmesan Vinaigrette (recipe follows)

Remove the tough outer leaves from the radicchio and trim a thin slice from the bottom of the core; discard. Pull off the remaining leaves, wash in cold water; pat dry with paper towels. Divide the radicchio among 4 plates; drizzle with the vinaigrette.

Per serving: 61 Calories, 4 g Total Fat, 1 g Saturated Fat, 4 mg Total Cholesterol, 101 mg Sodium, 3 g Total Carbohydrate, 1 g Dietary Fiber, 2 g Protein, 69 mg Calcium.

POINTS PER SERVING: 1

Tip

Drizzle leftover Crumbled Parmesan Vinaigrette on thick slices of day-old bread—the vinaigrette soaks into the bread, which gets wonderfully flavorful and softened.

Crumbled Parmesan Vinaigrette

Makes 4 servings

2 tablespoons balsamic vinegar
2 teaspoons extra virgin olive oil
¼ cup crumbled Parmesan cheese
Freshly ground pepper, to taste

In a small jar with a lid, shake the vinegar and oil. Add the cheese and pepper; shake again.

Per serving: 50 Calories, 4 g Total Fat, 1 g Saturated Fat, 4 mg Cholesterol, 94 mg Sodium, 2 g Total Carbohydrate, 0 g Dietary Fiber, 2 g Protein, 69 mg Calcium.

POINTS PER SERVING: 1

Tip

The older the Parmesan, the better it crumbles. Be sure you use authentic Parmigiano-Reggiano that's been aged at least 2 years when you make this robust and flavorsome dressing.

Strawberry-Rhubarb Compote

Makes 4 servings

1 cup orange juice
¼ cup sugar
2 cups diagonally sliced rhubarb (1″ pieces)
1 teaspoon grated orange zest
2 cups sliced strawberries

In a medium saucepan over medium heat, mix the orange juice and sugar, stirring until the sugar dissolves. Stir in the rhubarb and orange zest; bring just to a boil. Reduce the heat and simmer until the rhubarb is tender, about 5 minutes. Stir in the strawberries.

Per serving: 112 Calories, 0 g Total Fat, 0 g Saturated Fat, 0 mg Cholesterol, 3 mg Sodium, 27 g Total Carbohydrate, 3 g Dietary Fiber, 1 g Protein, 69 mg Calcium.

POINTS PER SERVING: 2

Tip

Strawberries and rhubarb are a classic pair, and even though spring is when they're both in season, we love this robust flavor combination in winter, too. Just use the frozen varieties when fresh are scarce.

A Poolside Lunch

My Mum is the most beautiful, most brilliant woman I have ever known. When Dads was consumed with his polo, we'd be left to Mum, who organized our ski trips abroad, the family holidays and the most wonderful birthday parties. She would instigate parties for my friends: swimming, ice-skating or to the movies or circus.

Mum would frequently bring Jane and me to one of our favorite childhood places to eat in London, Fortnum & Mason, where mayonnaise ruled supreme. My lunch order seldom varied: ham salad, then "three in a boat," a wonderful treat that consisted of one scoop each of mandarin, raspberry and lemon sorbet with raspberries and mandarin oranges.

Although my luncheon menus—and tastes!—have grown, I still look back on those days with fond memories. Not so much for the food, but for the time I spent with Mum and Jane. Nowadays, I work hard at creating great memories for my daughters.

Serves 4

Watermelon Slush
Summer Vegetable Salad with Sirloin Tips
Spicy Pita Chips
Fresh Blueberries with Sliced Mango and Kiwi*

Watermelon Slush

Makes 4 servings

4½ cups seedless watermelon chunks
2 tablespoons fresh lemon juice
1 tablespoon chopped mint
2–3 ice cubes
Fresh mint sprigs, to garnish

In a blender, combine the watermelon, lemon juice, mint and ice cubes; puree. Pour into 4 tall glasses; garnish with the mint sprigs.

Per serving: 60 Calories, 1 g Total Fat, 0 g Saturated Fat, 0 mg Cholesterol, 4 mg Sodium, 14 g Total Carbohydrate, 1 g Dietary Fiber, 1 g Protein, 16 mg Calcium.

POINTS PER SERVING: 1

Tip

For a refreshing summertime cocktail, add ½ cup chilled vodka.

Summer Vegetable Salad with Sirloin Tips

Makes 4 servings

2 tablespoons fresh lemon juice
2 tablespoons orange juice
1 tablespoon chopped rosemary
1 tablespoon extra virgin olive oil
1 garlic clove, minced
½ teaspoon freshly ground pepper
¼ teaspoon salt
1½ cups thinly sliced cooked sirloin steak
1 red bell pepper, seeded and slivered
1 medium zucchini, thinly sliced
½ red onion, thinly sliced
4 cups torn assorted salad greens

1. In a small bowl, whisk the lemon juice, orange juice, rosemary, oil, garlic, pepper and salt.
2. In a large bowl, mix the steak, bell pepper, zucchini and onion. Drizzle with the dressing; toss to combine. Refrigerate, covered, until chilled, at least 1 hour.
3. Divide the greens among 4 salad plates. Top with the steak mixture.

Per serving: 237 CALORIES, 10 G TOTAL FAT, 3 G SATURATED FAT, 76 MG CHOLESTEROL, 198 MG SODIUM, 9 G TOTAL CARBOHYDRATE, 3 G DIETARY FIBER, 28 G PROTEIN, 66 MG CALCIUM.

POINTS PER SERVING: 5

Tip

If you're interested in saving fat calories, roasted chicken breast without the skin can be substituted for the sirloin.

Spicy Pita Chips

Makes 4 servings

¾ teaspoon salt
¼–½ teaspoon cayenne pepper
4 large pitas or flour tortillas, cut into wedges

1. Preheat the oven to 350° F; line a baking sheet with foil, then spray with nonstick cooking spray.
2. In a small bowl, combine the salt and cayenne. Spray the pitas with nonstick cooking spray (olive-oil flavored is nice), sprinkle with the spice blend and place on the baking sheet in a single layer. Bake 15 minutes, then turn off the oven; let the pitas cool in the oven until crispy.

Per serving: 166 Calories, 1 g Total Fat, 0 g Saturated Fat, 0 mg Cholesterol, 722 mg Sodium, 34 g Total Carbohydrate, 1 g Dietary Fiber, 5 g Protein, 54 mg Calcium.

POINTS PER SERVING: 3

Tip

Try ¼–½ teaspoon flavored spice mix (like fajita or Cajun) instead of the cayenne for a slightly subtler taste.

Afternoon Tea

A typical British tea used to be traditional in some households. It included cucumber sandwiches, sausage rolls, butterfly cakes, which are little sponge cakes, and scones with cream and jam. A high tea is a cross between a tea and a light dinner and is usually served to children. It would include all of the above plus fish sticks and peas.

In my darkest days, tea with the children was one of the highlights of the day, as I relished the thought of all those comforts laid out before me. Tea is still important for us. Now, I know that I can enjoy some of these treats if they are made in a healthier way. Yet if I am served a regular tea, I simply watch the girls and sip my tea—willing myself not to reach out and overindulge. This tea menu has been adjusted to suit more American tastes.

Serves 8

Open-Face Ham Sandwiches

Cucumber Sandwiches

Blackberry Scones

Almond Biscotti

Pear-Port Quick Bread

Chocolate Mousse Tartlets

Open-Face Ham Sandwiches

Makes 8 servings

Eight ½″ slices French baguette
4 teaspoons Dijon mustard
4 paper-thin slices Parma ham (about 2 ounces), cut in half crosswise
½ pound buffalo mozzarella, cut into 8 slices
8 large basil leaves

Coat the baguette slices with the mustard. Layer each with the ham and mozzarella, then top with a basil leaf.

Per serving: 159 CALORIES, 7 G TOTAL FAT, 4 G SATURATED FAT, 22 MG CHOLESTEROL, 342 MG SODIUM, 14 G TOTAL CARBOHYDRATE, 1 G DIETARY FIBER, 9 G PROTEIN, 170 MG CALCIUM.

POINTS PER SERVING: 4

Tip

Parma ham is the authentic prosciutto di Parma, until recently unavailable in the United States. Buffalo mozzarella (sometimes called mozzarella *di bufala*) is indeed made from the milk of water buffalo; it is sweeter than the far more common cow's-milk mozzarella, with a deeper, richer flavor. If you can't find it, substitute fresh cow's-milk mozzarella.

Cucumber Sandwiches

Makes 8 servings

¼ cup reduced-fat blue cheese dressing
8 slices pumpernickel cocktail bread (3″ squares)
½ cucumber, peeled, seeded and sliced paper-thin
4 large dill sprigs

Spread the dressing on the bread. Top with the cucumber slices and a dill sprig.

Per serving: 34 CALORIES, 1 G TOTAL FAT, 0 G SATURATED FAT, 0 MG CHOLESTEROL, 160 MG SODIUM, 5 G TOTAL CARBOHYDRATE, 1 G DIETARY FIBER, 1 G PROTEIN, 17 MG CALCIUM.

POINTS PER SERVING: 1

Tip

To seed a cucumber easily, cut it in half lengthwise and run the tip of a spoon down the center, scooping out the seeds. The firmer and denser the bread, the better. For variety, substitute any creamy reduced-fat salad dressing for the blue cheese dressing.

Blackberry Scones

Makes 12 servings

1½ cups rolled oats

1½ cups all-purpose flour

⅓ cup sugar

1 tablespoon baking powder

½ teaspoon baking soda

½ teaspoon salt

½ cup (1 stick) cold reduced-calorie margarine,
cut into small pieces

¾ cup low-fat (1%) buttermilk

3 tablespoons seedless blackberry all-fruit spread

2 tablespoons fat-free egg substitute

1. Preheat the oven to 375° F; lightly spray a baking sheet with nonstick cooking spray.

2. In a food processor, combine the oats, flour, sugar, baking powder, baking soda and salt; whirl until the oats are finely ground, about 1 minute. Add the margarine and pulse until coarsely granular, about 40 times. With the machine running, drizzle the buttermilk through the feed tube to form a dough.

3. On a floured surface, turn out the dough. With lightly floured hands, pat it into a 10 x 8″ rectangle about ½″ thick. With the side of your finger, make a shallow spiral-shaped furrow in the dough; fill with the fruit spread, then gently press the fruit spread into the furrow. With a 2½″ biscuit or cookie cutter dipped in flour, cut out 12 scones, pushing the dough scraps together for the last. Transfer the scones to the baking sheet and brush the tops with egg substitute. Bake until golden, about 12 minutes. Cool on wire racks.

Per serving: 161 CALORIES, 5 G TOTAL FAT, 1 G SATURATED FAT, 1 MG CHOLESTEROL, 452 MG SODIUM, 26 G TOTAL CARBOHYDRATE, 1 G DIETARY FIBER, 4 G PROTEIN, 120 MG CALCIUM.

POINTS PER SERVING: 3

Tip

If available, use Irish steel-cut oats; they'll add a pleasantly chewy texture to these dense, moist scones. Wrap any leftovers for breakfast.

Almond Biscotti

Makes 36 servings

3 cups all-purpose flour

⅔ cup sugar

1 ½ teaspoons baking powder

¼ teaspoon salt

½ cup almonds, coarsely chopped

1 cup fat-free egg substitute

⅓ cup honey

1 teaspoon almond extract

1. Preheat the oven to 350° F; line a baking sheet with parchment, or line it with foil or wax paper and spray with nonstick cooking spray.
2. In a sifter or large strainer, combine the flour, sugar, baking powder and salt; sift into a large bowl. Stir in the almonds. In a medium bowl, whisk the egg substitute, honey and almond extract. Add to the dry ingredients, stirring to combine. Set aside about 5 minutes.
3. On a lightly floured surface, divide the dough in half and form into two 10 x 3″ logs. Transfer to the baking sheet. Bake until the logs are golden and beginning to crack on top, about 30 minutes. Remove from the oven and let cool about 10 minutes.
4. With a serrated knife, cut the loaves into ½″ slices, making 36 biscotti. Lay the slices flat onto the baking sheet. Bake the biscotti until dry and lightly toasted, about 10 minutes on each side. Cool completely on wire racks. Store in an airtight container.

Per cookie: 71 CALORIES, 1 G TOTAL FAT, 0 G SATURATED FAT, 0 MG CHOLESTEROL, 43 MG SODIUM, 14 G TOTAL CARBOHYDRATE, 0 G DIETARY FIBER, 2 G PROTEIN, 16 MG CALCIUM.

POINTS PER COOKIE: 2

For slightly chewier biscotti, in Step 4, stand the biscotti upright and toast for a total of 15 minutes. Stored in an airtight container, biscotti will keep 1–2 months.

Pear-Port Quick Bread

Makes 12 servings

6 ounces dried pears, chopped
¼ cup tawny port
2½ cups bread flour
¾ cup sugar
1 tablespoon baking powder
1 teaspoon baking soda
¼ teaspoon salt
1 cup low-fat (1%) buttermilk
¼ cup fat-free egg substitute
1 tablespoon reduced-calorie margarine, melted

1. In a small bowl, combine the pears and port. Preheat the oven to 350° F; lightly spray a 9″ loaf pan with nonstick cooking spray, then lightly dust it with flour.

2. In a sifter or large strainer, combine the flour, sugar, baking powder, baking soda and salt; sift into a large bowl. In a medium bowl, whisk the buttermilk, egg substitute and margarine until frothy. Add to the dry ingredients, stirring with a wooden spoon to combine. Stir in the pears and their soaking liquid. Transfer the dough to the loaf pan. Bake until the loaf begins to pull away from the edges of the pan and a tester inserted into the center of the loaf comes out clean, 50–60 minutes. Cool on a wire rack.

Per serving: 208 CALORIES, 1 G TOTAL FAT, 0 G SATURATED FAT, 1 MG CHOLESTEROL, 292 MG SODIUM, 45 G TOTAL CARBOHYDRATE, 1 G DIETARY FIBER, 5 G PROTEIN, 117 MG CALCIUM.

POINTS PER SERVING: 4

For variety, fold in ½ cup chopped pecans along with the pears. To make 3 mini loaves, divide the dough among three 5¾″ loaf pans and reduce the baking time by about 10 minutes. Toast any leftovers for breakfast.

Chocolate Mousse Tartlets

Makes 12 servings

¼ cup + 2 tablespoons sugar

1 egg white

⅛ teaspoon cream of tartar

1½ ounces unsweetened chocolate, melted

12 mini phyllo dough shells, at room temperature

1. In a small saucepan over medium heat, combine ¼ cup of the sugar and 2 tablespoons water; cook, swirling the pan periodically to dissolve the sugar, until the syrup reaches a temperature of 240° F, 8–9 minutes.
2. Meanwhile, in a large bowl with an electric mixer on low speed, beat the egg white until frothy. Add the cream of tartar and the remaining 2 tablespoons of sugar and beat at medium-high speed until stiff, glossy peaks form.
3. When the syrup reaches 240° F, beat it into the egg-white mixture at medium-high speed, mixing until the bowl is no longer hot. With a rubber spatula, fold in the chocolate. Spoon 1 tablespoon of the mousse into each phyllo shell. Refrigerate, covered, for 1 hour before serving.

Per serving: 72 CALORIES, 3 G TOTAL FAT, 1 G SATURATED FAT, 0 MG CHOLESTEROL, 51 MG SODIUM, 12 G TOTAL CARBOHYDRATE, 1 G DIETARY FIBER, 1 G PROTEIN, 4 MG CALCIUM.

POINTS PER SERVING: 1

Tip

Look for phyllo dough shells in the freezer case of supermarkets; they need not be cooked, only thawed. Heating the sugar syrup to 240° F (candy makers call this the soft-ball stage) cooks the egg-white mixture sufficiently to kill any bacteria. If you don't have a candy thermometer, drop a little of the syrup into a glass of cold water. It should form a ball that, when lifted out of the water, flattens slightly.

A Girlfriends' Get-Together

I have been fortunate to have some of the most extraordinary friends. My good friend Charlotte set off with me on a New World journey that took us from Rio to San Francisco. The two of us—18 years old and broke—finally landed in Squaw Valley in the high Sierras, and quickly secured a variety of odd jobs: we cleaned lavatories at our youth hostel, carried disabled children up the mountain and skied down with them and made strudel at the local bakery. I got huge from eating too much strudel, but the memory of it all still brings a smile to my face.

We were young and fearless! Full of energy and a sense of adventure. As I have grown older, I constantly try to learn from the mistakes I have made. Yet I also want to hold on to some of the bravery and fearlessness possessed by that young redhead.

Serves 4

Roast Chicken Salad (with Afghani bread)
Beet and Apple "Napoleon"
Chardonnay*

Roast Chicken Salad

Makes 4 servings

1 tablespoon olive oil

1 red bell pepper, seeded and finely diced

1 carrot, peeled and shredded

2 garlic cloves, minced

¼ teaspoon crushed red pepper flakes

2 cups shredded roast chicken breast

¼ cup fresh lemon juice

6 large green olives, pitted and sliced

8 arugula or radicchio leaves

1. In a medium nonstick skillet, heat the oil. Sauté the bell pepper, carrot, garlic and pepper flakes until the bell pepper is softened and the garlic is lightly golden, 1–2 minutes. Remove from the heat; stir in the chicken, lemon juice and olives.
2. Divide the arugula among 4 salad plates; top with the chicken mixture.

Per serving: 165 CALORIES, 7 G TOTAL FAT, 1 G SATURATED FAT, 48 MG CHOLESTEROL, 115 MG SODIUM, 9 G TOTAL CARBOHYDRATE, 2 G DIETARY FIBER, 19 G PROTEIN, 61 MG CALCIUM.

POINTS PER SERVING: 3

Tip

Turkey breast substitutes for chicken easily in this recipe, as does slivered celery in place of the carrot. Serve this robust salad with Afghani bread or pocketless pita (available at supermarkets or specialty stores).

Beet and Apple "Napoleon"

Makes 4 servings

4 beets
1 red onion, thinly sliced
2 tablespoons cider vinegar
1 Granny Smith apple, cored and thinly sliced into rings
1 tablespoon chopped parsley

1. Preheat the oven to 400° F. Trim the greens from the beets, leaving 1" of greens; save the greens for another use. Scrub the beets, then wrap in foil. Bake until a tester pierces the beets easily, 1¼–1½ hours. Remove the foil and let the beets cool enough to handle. Hold the beets under cold running water so the skins will slip off; you may have to rub gently. Thinly slice the beets and, in a medium bowl, combine them with the onion and vinegar. Refrigerate, covered, until chilled, at least 1 hour.

2. On each of 4 plates, layer the beets and onion with the apples; sprinkle with the parsley.

Per serving: 51 Calories, 0 g Total Fat, 0 g Saturated Fat, 0 mg Cholesterol, 44 mg Sodium, 12 g Total Carbohydrate, 3 g Dietary Fiber, 1 g Protein, 17 mg Calcium.

POINTS PER SERVING: 0

Tip

For the most attractive presentation, choose beets and apples that are about the same size in diameter.

A Midday Snack

The most soul-searching and difficult book I have authored has to be my autobiography, *My Story*. The book forced me to collect the emotions and thoughts I had amassed over my lifetime and try to put them into words, words that didn't always show me in a flattering light for the world to see. In retrospect, however, the book was a triumphant release. It marked a new beginning in my life: a fresh start for feeling better about myself and about my body.

In my travels across America, I have met many Weight Watchers members who have made their own fresh starts. From San Francisco and Denver to Chicago and New York, I have met new friends who share an old problem. Their courage to talk about their weight and how it has affected their lives is tremendous.

I am learning how to confront my issues with food. Taking a cue from the people I have met in the States, I try to use my new habits when dealing with my old problems. Now, if it's midday and I'm famished, I don't wait until I am out of control, which can lead to bingeing. If I have had a particularly trying and exhausting day, I enjoy a plate of fresh fruit with Parma ham and shavings of Parmesan. I also enjoy raw vegetables and a low-fat dip. All good, healthy foods that can keep me going.

Serves 4

Assorted Breadsticks*
Parma Ham and Honeydew Wedges with
Parmesan Shavings*
Platter of Crudités*
White Bean-Basil Dip
Roasted Red Pepper Dip

Dining with The Duchess
202

White Bean–Basil Dip

Makes 4 servings

One 19-ounce can white beans, rinsed and drained
⅓ cup coarsely chopped basil
3 tablespoons fresh lemon juice
4 teaspoons extra virgin olive oil
1 large garlic clove, peeled
½ teaspoon salt

In a blender or food processor, combine all the ingredients; puree. Let stand at room temperature, covered, until the flavors are blended, 2–3 hours.

Per serving: 193 CALORIES, 5 G TOTAL FAT, 1 G SATURATED FAT, 0 MG CHOLESTEROL, 643 MG SODIUM, 28 G TOTAL CARBOHYDRATE, 7 G DIETARY FIBER, 10 G PROTEIN, 70 MG CALCIUM.

POINTS PER SERVING: 3

Tip

This Tuscan-inspired dip is delicious with crusty bread, or try it with Spicy Pita Chips (page 188).

Roasted Red Pepper Dip

Makes 4 servings

2 red bell peppers
2 teaspoons tomato paste
2 teaspoons balsamic vinegar
1 garlic clove
⅛ teaspoon cayenne pepper

1. Line a baking sheet with foil; preheat the broiler. Place the peppers on the baking sheet; broil, turning frequently with tongs, until the skin is lightly charred on all sides, about 10 minutes. Transfer the peppers to a paper bag; fold the bag closed and let the peppers steam 10 minutes.
2. Fit a strainer over a small bowl. Peel the peppers over the strainer, removing and discarding the stems and seeds, allowing the juices to drip into the bowl.
3. In a food processor, combine the peppers and pepper juice with the remaining ingredients; puree until almost smooth.

Per serving: 22 CALORIES, 0 G TOTAL FAT, 0 G SATURATED FAT, 0 MG CHOLESTEROL, 4 MG SODIUM, 5 G TOTAL CARBOHYDRATE, 1 G DIETARY FIBER, 1 G PROTEIN, 7 MG CALCIUM.

POINTS PER SERVING: 0

Tip

Dollop any leftover dip on a baked potato or fresh steamed asparagus.

Wining and Dining

You don't have to have a wine cellar, spend hours at wine tastings or live in France to appreciate wine. Today, many of the stodgy "rules" of wine appreciation are obsolete: gone is the notion that white wine only goes with chicken or fish and red wine with meat. Today, wine experts acknowledge two principles: A good wine—regardless of whether it is red, white or blush—simply makes good food better, and when it comes to wine, pricier does not necessarily mean better. (Plenty of exceptional wines can be found for as little as ten dollars.)

Be adventurous with wine. Experiment by asking your local wine merchant or, when eating out, the sommelier (who is responsible for choosing the wines on the restaurant's menu) for his or her favorites. Keep the following tips in mind:

1. As a general rule, serve white and blush wines chilled to about 45° F by refrigerating or immersing in an ice bucket for about 30 minutes. The same rule is true for sparkling wines, which may also be served colder still. Red wines can be served cool (55° to 65° F) by placing the bottle in the refrigerator for a short period—about 20 minutes. A good rule of thumb: the simpler the wine, the more it will benefit from being chilled.

2. Don't be intimidated when tasting wine at a restaurant. Follow this protocol and you will impress even the stuffiest sommelier: First, observe the color and clarity of the wine (older wines often have a duller color than do young wines). Next, swirl the wine in the glass to release the aromas and the bouquet—the smell should be pleasing and aid in your appreciation of the wine. Now sip the wine, holding a small amount in your mouth; roll it around. Note if it's tart, sweet or bitter, or all of the above. These observations constitute the most important elements of wine appreciation—an experience you will likely want to build on. One point about tasting wine in a restaurant: Unless the wine is spoiled, which is extremely rare, returning a wine is generally not accepted.

3. Drink wine from the proper glass. An all-purpose wineglass will do the job, but the right glass makes for an even more captivating experience. White-wine glasses have tall, narrow bowls while red-wine glasses are large and rounded.

4. Unless you're a wine collector, you probably do not need a wine cellar, but you should still store wines properly. To store small amounts of wine for less than a year, simply keep the bottles on their sides where they won't be disturbed at a fairly stable temperature and out of direct sunlight.

5. To open a bottle of wine: First cut the plastic or metal wrapper (the capsule) covering the cork well below the lip of the bottle. Next, insert the corkscrew and pull to remove the cork. Wipe the lip of the bottle to remove any deposits left from the capsule or cork—pour and enjoy!

The following chart is a primer for the best-selling wines in the United States. Use it as your starting point for developing an appreciation of wines. Cheers!

Some Popular Varieties of Wine	Description	Try With
White		
Chardonnay	Dry, with an appealing balance of fruit, acidity and texture.	Red Snapper Primavera; Gorgonzola and Pear Pizza
Sauvignon Blanc	Grassy, herbal flavors.	Roast Chicken and Chutney Tea Sandwiches
Chenin Blanc	Light and well-balanced with a fresh delicate floral character.	Open-Face Ham Sandwiches; Cider Pork Chops
Gewürztraminer	Spicy aroma and full flavors; range from dry to sweet.	Barbecue Beef Sandwiches

Some Popular Varieties of Wine	Description	Try With
White Riesling	Floral, with fruity-yet-delicate aromas and flavors.	Parma Ham and Honeydew Wedges; Mushroom-Caraway Soup
Red		
Cabernet Sauvignon	Full-bodied, rich, intense wine with cherry-currant, sometimes herbal, flavors and noticeable tannins.	Roasted Pork Loin; Lamb Chops with Mint Salsa
Merlot	Medium- to full-bodied red with herbaceous flavors.	Classic Roast Beef; Chicken Calvados
Pinot Noir	Light- to medium-bodied red that is delicate, smooth and rich in complexity.	Provençal Beef Tenderloin
Zinfandel	Light-, medium- or full-bodied; rich in berrylike — sometimes spicy — flavors.	Steak Frites
Blush		
White Zinfandel	Off-dry flavor.	Summer Vegetable Salad with Sirloin Tips; Mesquite Chicken Salad

*Information supplied by The Wine Institute, San Francisco, CA.

Index